My Thirteenth Winter

A MEMOIR

SAMANTHA ABEEL

SCHOLASTIC INC.
New York Toronto London Auckland Sydney
Mexico City New Delhi Hong Kong Buenos Aires

ALSO BY SAMANTHA ABEEL
Reach for the Moon

∿

ACKNOWLEDGMENTS

I would like to thank the following individuals for filling my life with love, friendship, wisdom, joy, and distraction, and without whom this book would never have been possible: Don and Nancy Tubesing, Amy Griffin, and Sven Birkerts, for all of your hard work, encouragement, wisdom, help, and guidance, and for believing in me and this project. This book is because of you. Danny Siegel, Naomi Eisenberger, Ranya Kelly, Marc and Arleen Sternfeld, and Sharon Halper, for being a second family and for all of your caring, summer after summer. Phoebe Hazzard, Anica Rushing, Vanessa Arseneau, and Laura Feeney, for being uncommon women in my life and my M.H.C. sisters! Thank you for all your support and caring. To all of my teachers, since without you none of this would have been possible. Roberta Williams and Charlie Murphy, for helping me reach for the moon, and for your continued support and encouragement. W. Scott Herron, Sean Thomas, Brett Becker, and the boys of Hemingway House 2000–2002 who celebrated this book's beginning. Thank you for all your good wishes and patience. Christine Sherrod and Erin Wade, thank you for your friendship, encouragement, and senses of humor, and for putting up with me while I completed this project. Dave Speckman, Murray, and McGee, thank you for being there for the tears and laughter, and for fetching all the sticks and stones I have thrown. J. Christine Whalen, you allowed me to enter those dark places and you never let go of my hand. Mom, Dad, Zac, and Otis Abeel, you have all been my anchor and I can't believe how lucky I am to belong to you!

FOR

DON AND NANCY TUBESING

THIS STORY COULD NOT HAVE BEEN TOLD WITHOUT YOU

THANK YOU FOR GIVING ME WINGS

J. CHRISTINE WHALEN

THANK YOU FOR YOUR WISDOM, INSIGHT, AND CARING

YOU ALLOWED ME TO ENTER THOSE DARK PLACES AND

NEVER LET GO OF MY HAND

DANNY SIEGEL

YOU CONTINUE TO BE ONE OF MY LIFE'S GREATEST TEACHERS

AND

ELIZABETH, DAVID, ZAC, AND OTIS ABEEL

FOR YOUR UNCONDITIONAL LOVE

Introduction

I am twenty-five years old and I can't tell time. I struggle with dialing phone numbers, counting money, balancing my checkbook, tipping at restaurants, following directions, understanding distances, and applying basic math to my everyday life. I also struggle with spelling and grammar, and remembering combinations of movements in athletics and dance. I cannot read a note of music, even though I've participated in choir since elementary school.

I have been diagnosed with *dyscalculia*, a learning disability that affects my capacity to learn skills based on sequential processing, such as math, spelling, and grammar. Living with a learning disability has created many challenges, and I have often felt frustrated, confused, and alone.

However, my learning disability has also afforded me a unique view of the world and has taught me some important lessons. It has forced me to always look for, and be open to, creative solutions, and not to take even the simplest of tasks for granted. Through the many individuals that have helped me in my life, I have witnessed the full meaning of compassion and empathy, and it is because of them that I now move in currents of self-discovery and possibility. My learning disability has taught me always to look for potential and to see people as beautiful individuals waiting for their gifts to be recognized. I have come to see everyone as learning disabled and gifted.

This book was written as a celebration of the simultaneous brilliance and imperfection that comes with being human.

Before the Labels

SOMETIMES I TRY TO GO

back and remember the me

before I was ever diagnosed with

a learning disability, back before

I ever knew I was different, back

to the time when I was just

me, without any labels, when I

thought the way I saw the world

was how everyone saw it.

As a child growing up, I looked like any other kid in my neighborhood. I was enthusiastic, inquisitive, and interested in just about everything. I laughed easily, and was creative and eager to learn. Looking at early photos of myself — dark hair and eyes staring out of a round face, squatting to look at rocks, holding my mom's hand for balance as I toddled down the sidewalk, curled up on my dad's lap while he read to me, playing in the mud with my little brother Zac — nobody would have been able to predict my life would fall apart during my thirteenth winter.

Like most kids, I went off to kindergarten, cautiously excited about the new adventure. I remember Eliza with her brown braids and wanting her to be my friend. I remember being in love with my teacher and desperately wanting her approval. I also remember wanting to stand out, wanting attention for my intelligence and for what I knew. I was always trying to come up with the most creative or advanced answer I could to questions my teacher asked in class — sometimes using knowledge I had overheard or gathered from my parents' conversations. I remember one time feeling particularly proud of my answer when my teacher introduced a new letter of the alphabet to our class.

I want to be near the front, but I know Mrs. Boerma does not like people rushing and pushing. She stands beside the fireplace and calls us over in clusters from our desks to the floor surrounding her enormous rocking chair. I am quiet and very still as I wait my turn. She calls on my cluster, and I calmly walk toward the front of the room while Richie and Michael rush toward her chair, pushing their way in a wild attempt to see who can get closest to the front. I sit cross-legged on the blue carpeting flecked with green and run my hands over the Brillo-y surface, feeling particles of sand stick to my palms. I am on the outside of the crescent of bodies. It is a long, high-ceilinged room, filled with light coming through big tall wide windows. Mrs. Boerma sits in her rocking chair, and she is the kindest, most beautiful person in the world. All I want is to be close to her, to get approval from her. I want her to like me.

Mrs. Boerma holds up a balloon with a colorful character on it that incorporates a letter from the alphabet, one of the new Letter People. The whole class presses forward to see it. The new Letter Person is the letter N. Mrs. Boerma asks us to name as many things as we can think of that start with the letter N. Hands shoot up. "Noodle." "Nut." "Nurse." Each one is defined and then sounded out, "Nnnnoodle," emphasizing the new letter sound. "Good," she says and moves on to the next word.

I think hard; I want to say a word no one else has said, a word no one else would think of. I have it. I raise my hand, she calls on me. "Neumonia," I say. All eyes look at me and then at Mrs. Boerma to get her reaction. My eyes never leave her face. "Well, that is an interesting word. Does anyone know what that word means?" Everyone is silent. I know the answer but it feels wrong for me to say it, other kids don't like know-it-alls. Mrs. Boerma explains that it is an illness that can make it hard for a person to breathe. "However," she goes on to say, "pneumonia is actually spelled with a P, even though it sounds like it has an N in front of it." PNEUMONIA, she writes it out for us to see on her easel pad. "It's a confusing word because it is not spelled the way it sounds. But you are right, Sam, it does have an Nnnn *sound in it." She sends that slight smile my way again, and I feel warm and victorious as she asks for two more words that begin with N.*

I am proud that I have come up with a word no one else knew about. Even though it doesn't begin with an N, it is still a word older people know. I feel glad that the other kids think of me as smart.

Along with enjoying my growing sense of identity as a "smart kid" and good student, I also enjoyed thinking about big ideas. I began to develop a fascination with time. Not in its number form, but time on a universal cosmic scale. Time in its unfathomable length measured in change. In first grade, I became obsessed with the idea that human beings were not always here and that millions and millions of years had passed before we ever arrived. It seemed so incredible to me, the concept of change on that grand a scale. Night after night I would make my dad pull out my favorite dinosaur books. Many were for adults, but I really just wanted to look at the pictures and dream and wonder how these giant lizards ever walked the earth. I drew pictures of dinosaurs and wrote about them in my reports. In our Thanksgiving cards we had to write what we were thankful for. I said I was thankful for my parents and for paleontology.

As I progressed through school, my fascination with dinosaurs diminished, but my need to stand out through my creativity and intelligence grew with each passing grade. In second grade, show-and-tell time provided the perfect opportunity.

"Sam, I believe it's your turn," I hear Mrs. Kendall's warm voice say

over the din of talking that erupts without fail in between each show-and-tell presentation. I take a deep breath and stand up. I can't tell if I feel nervous or excited about what I am going to share. I practiced it last night with my mom, but here, as I look out at the faces of my classmates and teacher, I don't know if I can pull it off. What I do know is that no one else has ever brought anything like this before.

I lift the paper grocery bag from the place where I am sitting and I move to the table in front of the class. I set the bag down and unroll the folded top. I look down, reach into the bag, and then pull my hands out quickly, saying, "Be nice and behave." Everyone in the class begins to lean in closer, curiosity spreading, all of them wondering what I have in my paper sack.

I place my hands back in the bag and after a little struggle, I pretend to lift something fairly heavy up and out of the sack. "This," I say to the class, "is my invisible pet dragon." A heavy silence falls upon my classmates, along with a few confused looks. "If you are all really good," I continue, "I will let him go so you can watch him fly around the room." More silence and wide, wide eyes.

I begin to describe my dragon to the class as a furry white mix of a puppy and a dragon. I tell them it has pointy colorful wings and big brown eyes and a long tail. As I describe it to the class, a vivid cartoony image fills my mind and I can see it there in full color, its cute face and spiky tail. "OK, I'm going to let him go now so he can fly around the room a little." I move my arms in imitation of someone releasing a bird, and I begin to narrate its flight—warning Amber to look out since it just went whizzing past her head, telling Steve to pet it since it just landed on his shoulder.

My classmates begin to laugh and shout, wanting him to land on their heads or requesting a chance to pet him. After a few minutes, I stretch out my arms and scoop them in toward my chest so that it looks as if I have caught my dragon in my arms. I tell him he is a good boy and pet him a little before I carefully lower him back into the bag and roll the top down.

Silence follows. I begin to feel a bit unsure and anxious about my show-and-tell success. Then hands begin to shoot up in the air. I answer their questions about what I feed him, where he sleeps at night, and where I found him. Mrs. Kendall sounds thrilled with my presentation and creativity. She thanks me for bringing in my pet, then begins to dismiss rows for recess.

I feel relieved that my performance is over and pleased that I took the risk. I quietly place my paper bag on the back table with the other show-and-tell items and sit down, waiting to be excused. I feel rewarded by the smiles of my friends and teacher, the whispers of "That was cool!" from some as they pass by my desk.

Hints of Trouble

EVEN THOUGH I FELT

proud of my identity as one of

the smart and creative kids in

school, my mom says that

something changed when I

started kindergarten. At first,

even she didn't notice it. I was

always outgoing and talkative at

home.

However, when she arrived for parent–teacher conferences, she was surprised to learn that at school I was behaving quite differently. The teachers said I was withdrawn, quiet, cautious, very reserved. I spent a lot of my free time watching everyone else in the class and was timid and slow at picking up new tasks. Mom was confused and asked me about it when she got home, but I didn't know what to say. I didn't realize there was such a dramatic difference.

Mom remembers that in first grade I would sometimes come home crying but I never had a reason. She would often ask me why, but she never got an answer. The only thing I can remember feeling bad about that year was my struggle with learning to read. I started out in one of the more advanced reading groups, but I was quickly moved to one of the slower groups after I began to flounder with mastering the skills. I was mortified by this move and for the first time I questioned my own confidence in my intelligence.

I also remember struggling with the concept of fractions in first grade. Each student in the class was given a Hershey chocolate bar. The teacher had each of us break our bar in half, and she explained that the two sections in front of us were one half of the whole. This made sense. However, as she continued to break up the bar into its divided parts, I became more and more confused. When one of the pieces was again broken in half, why was it called a quarter? How could a chocolate bar with three pieces in it be called one-fourth? I never figured it out or understood. Instead I ate the chocolate and decided it wasn't that important.

I don't recall exactly when the big struggle began. I assume there were little ones every day as I tried to complete each page of my math workbook. However, I do remember in second grade sitting around the teacher's big rocking chair while she manipulated the hands on her pretend clock. She would set the hands at a certain time and then ask us to tell her what time it was or whether it was a quarter to or half past. I remember feeling confused, uncomfortable, and not understanding any of it. It seemed like things were moving too fast, and I couldn't grasp the logic behind the answers given.

I also felt anxious about maintaining my identity. I felt very strongly that I did not want anyone to know I didn't get it, and that I should pretend I did. Everyone thought I was smart and I didn't want them thinking otherwise; I didn't want to think otherwise. However, my inability to live up to my label as a smart, creative student became more and more apparent to me as time passed and our math assignments grew in complexity.

My teacher, Mrs. Kendall, walks around the room, weaving in and out between our desks. A stack of photocopies is slung over one arm while with her other hand she pulls sheet after sheet from the pile and lays one in front of each student she passes. Like a falling white bird, my copy leaves her fingers and floats to its resting place on the empty fake-wood top of my desk. The paper is blank on the side that faces me, a perfect rectangle of white.

Mrs. Kendall finishes passing out the work sheets and makes her way to the front of the room. All eyes come to rest on her face and a serious silence falls over the class. "Now, as you know, this is a timed exercise," she says. "When I say go, you will all flip your papers over. You have two minutes to answer the problems on your sheet. Then, when you are done and have all of your problems correct, you will get to go to the back of the room and have ice cream."

Murmurs of excitement run through the group and all twenty-two pairs of eyes look to the back of the room, where the teacher's assistant sits opening bags of ice-cream cones and pulling lids off frozen buckets.

"Remember," Mrs. Kendall continues, "as soon as you're finished, you need to bring your paper up to me so I can look it over and make corrections if I need to."

There is a suspenseful pause and a shifting of body positions as everyone, sensing the time has arrived, comes to face squarely forward in their desks. Like runners taking their marks at a race, everyone sits, bows his or her head down, eyes falling to the white backs of their papers, waiting for the sound that will give them permission to start.

Mrs. Kendall's eyes sweep the room and mine do as well. I can feel my pulse quicken and my fingers press down on the flat sides of my pencil. I don't feel nervous about the problems waiting for me on the other side of the paper. I already know that I won't get all of them right but that doesn't bother me. Instead, I swallow hard and recognize the sickening feeling that I don't seem to get the obvious. During these timed math trials, everyone else can read the clock or has some secret sense of time that I lack completely. I will hear them whisper, "Only thirty seconds left." Or I'll see them looking up at the clock and back at their paper, using the clock as a tool to tell them how much time they still have.

My muscles tense, I bow my head, and I hear Mrs. Kendall say, "Go." A whipping sound fills the air as all the students flip their papers over and begin to answer the problems. I am conscious of heads bowed in focused concentration, of the whisper of lead on the papers' surfaces, of how quickly Andy's pencil moves, of how quickly all their pencils move. I look down at the blue lines of problems and begin to add as fast as I can. Problem after problem, everything fades out around me. Then sounds of racing feet disrupt me, and several pairs of eyes, including mine, watch Andy and Jeb rush to be first to Mrs. Kendall's desk to have their papers looked over.

If they are done, how much more time do we have? How much time did it take them? My eyes shift from my paper up to the big, black-rimmed, circular face of the clock that looms over the classroom from its perch above the door. It tells me nothing. I can name the numbers I see, and I know the hands that stretch out from its center are supposed to give me the answer I am looking for, but for me the direction that they point to doesn't mean anything. Panic and helplessness surge through me. I know I am running out of time, but I am unable to tell when the end will come and how much time I have left until it does. I feel completely disoriented, like I am falling through space without any beginning or end. It's like being left in a wide-open field without any markers or reference points, no edges in view to help guide me.

My eyes turn from the clock face to the faces I can read, those of my classmates. Steve sneaks a peek at the clock, and I see his pencil quicken. It won't be long now. I can tell by the way Mrs. Kendall shifts in her seat, glances at the clock, her lips moving slightly. I know she is counting. Time is running out.

I feel horrified and ashamed as the realization hits me: I am supposed to be able to read clocks by now; my peers can all tell time and I can't. What's wrong with me? I go back to work on my problems, but I feel weighed down with the guilt of a dark secret, something I have to keep hidden. As each wave of kids finishes their papers, I begin to feel more and more weight and pressure. My stomach tightens as I anticipate the sickening feeling of being the last one to finish.

The two minutes come and go. There are three of us left. Then one finishes. I look up and see the group in the back of the room crowding around the table with their ice cream. I don't really care about the ice cream, but I do care about how it looks for me to still be hashing out math problems at my desk so long after almost the entire class has finished. I finish, along with the other remaining girl, and walk up to the teacher's desk.

Mrs. Kendall takes my paper with a kind, encouraging smile. I watch as she checks off my problems. Some I have added when the sign said to subtract. Others I have subtracted when I was supposed to add. In some, I forgot to include certain numbers. My answers aren't anywhere close to correct. Mrs. Kendall points out these errors, goes over them, asks me to go back and make corrections. I do so, trying to block out the joyful chatting of the rest of the class and pretending I am invisible, hoping they won't notice me: Sam, the smart girl, still at her desk.

I walk up to Mrs. Kendall's desk again and again, careful to maintain my outward calm and poise. Each time there are corrections to be made and some she has to talk me through. I go over my paper for the third time, sitting with her at her desk, and she whispers, "You can go over and have ice cream now. It's all right."

I am relieved to join the other kids, but somehow I don't feel right having ice cream. I haven't gotten the problems right. It's a prize that doesn't belong to me. I stick my spoon into the white melting stuff and can't feel any joy. I haven't earned it.

Trouble was starting to show up in other areas of my life as well. I had started piano lessons in second grade. I liked the idea of being able to play, but I started to dread going to lessons, since I always seemed to mess them up, even when I had practiced.

My piano teacher lived in a big, three-story house a few blocks away. Twice a week I walked to her house after school, my music books weighing down my backpack. The trip seemed longer every lesson. Eventually, I would reach her house, climb the stairs to her porch, and knock. I would step inside, then into the living room and take my place at the baby grand. She would sit beside me on the piano bench and ask me to perform the pieces I had practiced during the week, and then give me new ones to practice and music theory lessons to complete in the workbook. I came to hate playing the piano, but felt obligated to practice, not wanting to disappoint my teacher. I complained to my parents, but they were adamant that I continue.

Finally, one time my teacher sent me home with a note for my mom. Not long after that, my parents let me quit taking piano lessons. Later, my mom told me that my teacher had contacted her, expressing great concern. She said she had never seen anything like it. I would come to lessons, and she knew I had practiced the pieces. I would sit at the piano and play them beautifully. Then she would ask me to play the same piece again, and I would have to hack my way through it as if I had never seen it before. It was the same with my music theory. I just didn't get it. Even after she explained it several different ways. Later, we would discover that music and math abilities are closely linked.

My mom had heard from my teachers that I struggled with arithmetic, but it was not until one night during my second-grade year when we practiced with flash cards that she witnessed the reality of my disability for the first time. She thought she could teach me. She thought it must have been a matter of the way the material was explained in class. It was not until she tried to explain it to me herself that she began to understand there really was something wrong.

I sit cross-legged on the edge of my bed. My mom sits on my floor with the flash cards fanned out in front of her. I am bored with math in school and bored and disappointed that my mom has decided to make me practice it at home. She, however, is excited by the prospect of working on math with me.

The first card she holds up is $5 - 2 = \underline{\quad}$. I look at the card and its red-tinted symbols. I remember minus means to take away, but nothing else holds any meaning. My mind is a blank. I fight to compute the numbers but my brain feels as if it is searching through empty file cabinets. Mom sees the vacant look on my face.

Refusing to be ruffled, she assumes her best patient teacher attitude, clears her throat, and lays five cards down on the carpet. "Now, what happens when I take two of these away?" With a sweep of her hand two cards disappear. My brain struggles to retrieve the answer and comes up empty again. I take a tentative stab at it. "But now you have three cards," my voice hesitant and confused.

"Right, because . . ." Mom lifts her eyebrows, poised for an answer.

I don't know. I don't have an answer.

"Watch, I'll do it again," she says, still maintaining her patient confidence. Once again, my mom lays five cards in front of her. "OK, how many cards do I have in front of me?" I count them. "Five."

"Good. Now, how many do I have left after I take two away?"

"But now you have three cards," I say again, bewildered and confused. I honestly do not understand. I hear a subtle change in my mother's voice, something that makes it sound tighter, a little more forceful. She leans forward now, more intent. I move from my place on the edge of my bed down to the floor in front of her, separated from my mom by the red backs of the flash cards.

"The answer to five minus two is three. See, I had five cards and I took away two and now there are three cards left." I look at her again with my blank face. I hear her explanation and try to follow it, but can't attach any meaning to the words she uses. I don't follow her logic. She looks intently at my face for a moment, searching it for some sign that I understand what she is saying. But she finds none and, clearing her throat, she moves on to other problems.

She holds up other cards. Some I have memorized and give the correct answer immediately. Others I struggle with, and with each struggle comes an explanation from my mom, sometimes several, and after each failed attempt she becomes more tense, more intent.

Eventually, Mom decides to go back to the problem $5 - 2 = $ ____. She wears a look of determined expectation. "OK," she says. "Here is one you will get for sure." I look again at the symbols on the card and I feel my brain working, searching to access the information, but no answers come. "I don't know," I finally stammer out. "I don't know the answer."

"Slow down and think about it. We've gone over this." Once again, Mom demonstrates the concept with the cards. Once again, I watch and still don't understand. She directs another soliciting look at me, but this time I sense a change in my mother. There is frustration and desperation in her voice, and something that makes my stomach turn inside out. I see fear in her face and eyes, alarm as she watches me struggle and not find the answers. She is scared. For the first time, a new and terrible thought grips me. I realize that there is something wrong with me — something so wrong that it makes my mom afraid. I am afraid, too. I begin to cry.

"Come on Sam, you know you can get this. . . . It makes sense. . . ."

"I can't," I say through broken sobs. "I don't know." My mom begins to cry as well, her calm exterior broken.

My mom had just witnessed the phantom obstacle that I faced every day; the invisible entity my teachers had only caught glimpses of. She was alone with the realization that I was not normal, that it wasn't simply a matter of me not paying attention in class or the teacher's style of instruction. There really was something wrong with me.

As my second-grade year progressed, my teacher became more and more concerned at how far I seemed to be slipping behind the rest of the class in math. After my mom's experience working with me on flash cards, the school and my parents decided to have me evaluated for a learning disability. My mom explained their decision to me and said there wasn't anything wrong with me, it was just that I might have a crossed wire somewhere in my brain, and they were going to see if they could find it. I didn't mind being tested; in fact, it appealed to me. I liked the attention and showing adults what I could do. I saw it as a challenge.

Her high heels tap along the whole length of the long wide corridor, echoing rhythmically. I follow beside her, passing the wide, pale yellow lockers and, at equal intervals, open classroom doorways, revealing separate unique worlds of bustle and activity. She asks me a few questions along the way in a gentle kind voice, and I decide I like her. Mom said they wanted to have me tested, that I was a little behind in math, and they wanted to find out how I was doing overall.

We enter a small room, a quasi-office closet with a small table and two chairs. She sits in the big chair on one side of the table and I take the little one across from her. She takes out some notebooks from her bag, some cards, a pen, a flip book with colorful pictures, and some blocks. I feel confident and serious. I like tests. I like to show adults what I can do. I like the one-on-one attention, and leaving class in the middle of the day makes me feel important somehow.

We begin the test, which is made up of games and puzzles, questions and answers. At one point, she gives me a series of numbers in a pattern that I have to repeat back to her. She also gives me a group of wooden blocks I have to place in order, and pictures that I have to organize so they tell a story. I feel myself working hard to concentrate and pay attention. To do the best I can.

When we finish, she pulls out a glass jar full of bright-colored candy, tells me what a good job I have done, and lets me pick out a sucker to take with me. She walks me back to my classroom, and as I enter I hear whispers from the other students wondering where I have been, but they quickly fade as Mrs. Kendall begins to read another chapter from the story. I walk to my desk and take a seat, eager to listen, hoping I did well on the test.

I never heard much about the results of the test except that while my math scores were low I scored very high in other areas. They told my parents I qualified for both the special education and gifted programs. But since that dichotomy didn't make much sense, the school decided to keep me in a regular education class-room. My mom and dad were told not to worry, that I would eventually "even out." Trusting the school experts, my parents accepted their recommendation and hoped I would eventually catch up with the rest of my class in math.

Growing Difficulties

ONE OF OUR FIRST TASKS

in third grade was to learn the

multiplication tables. I was good

at memorization and quickly

acquired the ability to recite

the tables. My mom and teachers

thought my problems might be

solved because I appeared to

understand multiplication.

Everyone felt relieved — including me, because I, too, felt like I might actually be getting it.

However, their celebrations and sighs of relief were short lived. Soon after entering fourth grade the truth became apparent. While I could recite the numbers and the multiplication tables that I had memorized, they were only symbols with numerical names that didn't mean anything to me. I didn't understand the concepts behind them. Faced with the daily onslaught of progressively more difficult mathematical concepts, I could no longer deny there was a problem. I started to shut down completely. I found myself unable to cope, and for the first time I became clearly aware of the fact that I didn't get things my classmates did. I began to feel less and less comfortable at school. I felt anxious that someone would find out I couldn't understand everything. I always felt the most vulnerable during the math portion of the day.

My whole being is quiet, while everyone else in the classroom seems to move and buzz. Outwardly, I work to appear poised and calm. My lips feel straight, tight, and irrevocably closed against my teeth. I am careful to keep the lines around my eyes expressionless. I watch Mr. Mummert's hand move with swift confidence, dragging and tapping the pale yellow chalk across the blackboard. A series of symbols appears in his wake: the interesting dashes of a multiplication sign, a division symbol, two horizontal lines meaning equals, numbers set around these in an orderly fashion, each group leading to the next as Mr. Mummert's words and gestures confirm.

Inside I sink, flutter, and tighten. I open my eyes wider and try, even though I know it is impossible, to stretch the opening of my ears. I work at not allowing myself to blink, convinced I must have blinked when Mr. Mummert went over the key part of the problem, or my ears must have missed a key phrase that would tie all of this together. Looking at the yellow marks on the board, I feel as if I am staring into the face of someone I should know but can't seem to remember. No matter how hauntingly familiar the figures are, they continue to remain anonymous strangers and a wave of guilt and embarrassment moves through me.

The guilt grows, along with an anxious burning that smolders from my insides outward into my cheeks. I dart a look at the clearly comprehending faces of the rest of the class. I feel so far away from everyone, removed, alone in my ignorance. I am terrified there is something really wrong with me. I understand most of my other subjects, and math seems to be so easy for my classmates. I feel like a liar, as if I have been leading them on. I have made everyone believe that I am smart. The teachers all like me, I am a good artist, I am creative. It must seem like I am good at almost everything, but they don't know how lost I feel inside, how helpless. I feel weighed down by the idea that it is too late to say anything. I feel guilty for making it into the fourth grade without being able to consistently add or subtract. There are lots of things I didn't master along the way — I only pretended to. Was I supposed to tell someone the truth?

Terror begins to freeze up my entire frame as I realize that Mr. Mummert is going to call on someone for the final answer, that he is going to turn around and that he may call on me. There is a moment of silence as he makes a few last dashes with the chalk. Eager hands shoot up around me,

and there is a general squirming toward the edge of seats and a few whis-
pers: "I know . . . I know what the answer is." Mr. Mummert finishes and
turns around to face the class. I am paralyzed, frozen like my pet rabbit
when my dog walks past her cage in the yard. I drop my eyes away from Mr.
Mummert, careful not to attract any attention to myself. The words in my
head repeat themselves again and again as I hold my breath: Please don't
call on me. Please . . . don't . . . call . . . on . . . me.

"Elizabeth," he asks, "why don't you come up here and show us how you
got your answer." He hands her the chalk. I release the air I have been
holding in my chest and my muscles relax with relief, as I sink back in my
chair. For a few moments, while Elizabeth awkwardly scratches out her an-
swer, I am safe, until Mr. Mummert approaches the chalkboard again.

Every day this ritual was repeated. I felt scared and lonely. Math
wasn't the only problem. By fourth grade, my struggle with basic
spelling, as well as remembering the parts of a sentence and understanding basic grammar, became very apparent. I had come
to hate English. In earlier grades, English had been nothing but
copying sentence after sentence from a textbook and then searching for, circling, or adding whatever part of the sentence was required by that assignment. I was terrible at all of this. I couldn't
keep any of the details straight in my head. Each new rule would
confuse the last one, and then I'd mix them up.

My academic struggles also affected my social life. I began to
retreat, withdrawing into myself. I no longer raised my hand in
class. I rarely let myself feel free to play, except with a select few

friends on the playground. I didn't fit in with the rest of my class-mates. My thoughts and ideas seemed different from theirs. When we were given free time as a class, I often chose to stay at my desk alone, drawing or reading. Or I would wander over to the windows at the back of the classroom and look out or watch everyone else from that vantage point.

I began to comfort myself with thoughts that I was talented and smart, but before my time. I compared myself to heroines in fairy tales. I loved believing that I, like them, was misunderstood and that I was supposed to feel melancholy and alone. One day I would accomplish something special, something different.

I am sitting up on the long metal heater that runs underneath the tall windows at the back of my fourth-grade classroom. I lean back against the wall, my legs tucked into my chest. From this corner of the room I can watch everyone. Mr. Mummert is at his desk correcting papers and answering Sara's questions. Every so often, he raises his head and scans the room. I turn my head away from the class and look out through the windows over the wide front lawn of my elementary school at two or three tall old white pine trees that are taller than anything else on the block, with long, strong trunks and bristles of glistening needles at their ends. I try to imagine the row of houses across the street disappearing and everything, even the grass in front of me, covered with nothing but trees. Even my house, kitty-corner from the school, was nothing but a darkened patch of forest floor. An aching shiver goes through me as I think about the passing of so much time and what used to be.

Everything outside blurs as my eyes continue to look toward the window but my mind turns inward. It feels right to spend my free time up here, in the corner, alone. It is the way things are supposed to be, I reassure myself. I am supposed to be separate. The quiet virtuous heroine, wise beyond her years. I was meant to be misunderstood and different. Look at all of them. All they worry about is boys, clothes, hair, who is fastest, who is not. They act out, do what they are not supposed to. They don't listen, really listen, not even to one another. I have been chosen, instead, for something special. I am not meant to fit in. Things are supposed to be this way.

My classmates seemed to notice there was something different about me as well. One of the popular girls, who was always getting in trouble for being too loud or talking too much, used to tell me I was wise. We weren't friends. We never played together after school or hung out at recess, but if she had a problem and she wanted help, she would ask to sit with me at a separate table after we were done eating lunch. She would sit across from me and explain her dilemma — usually a friendship crisis or how she should handle a situation with a teacher.

At first, I felt strange giving her advice on situations, most of which I had never experienced myself. However, the answers or solutions always came easily for me and she always appeared to leave feeling enlightened. She expressed a bit of awe at my "wisdom." She called our meetings "counseling sessions."

Looking back, it is interesting that I was never chastised or made fun of for my introverted behavior. My classmates always afforded me a certain amount of respect. I remember this even as far back as kindergarten. I wasn't picked on. No one played tricks on me or threw snowballs at me. Instead, I was seen as smart and wise, not someone to ridicule.

During elementary school, home was where I truly came alive. Home was where I could be free to be myself. On weekends and after school, my friends and I would play for hours. Heather, Melissa, Nicole, Jenny, we would spend our time imagining and pretending. There was no truer feeling of joy or of all-consuming passion than when I had an opportunity to use my imagination in creative play.

The goal was to make things feel as real as possible using whatever we could find. We commandeered our parents' junk mail and pretended we were bankers, or played office. We pulled out maps and pretended we were travel agents, using younger siblings as customers. We pretended snowdrifts were giant icebergs and front porches were sailing ships or palaces. We put on plays and fashion shows for our parents. Choreographed dances. My back deck was transformed to the perfect make-believe house or theater stage.

Those hours of imaginative play were when I felt most absolutely, fully alive, every fiber of my being totally absorbed in the moment, no worries or fears for the future.

We are in desperate need of food and luckily our ship with the help of our pet humpback whales is going to land on the next island just in time. According to our charts, unfolded road maps from Heather's mother's car, we are due to see land at any moment. In preparation, Heather sweeps the planks of the ship while I look around for materials to rig a sink and cooking area. I select the place where there is a bend in the porch as the spot for our galley. Hanging an old putty bucket by its handle to a hook on one of the porch pillars, I am able to weave the hose up through the spokes in the porch railing and up the pillar so it hangs down and pours like a faucet into the bucket when it is turned on.

Our ship is fully equipped. We have bunk beds made out of two porch chairs set facing each other, old hanging flower baskets are used for food and specimen storage as well as for drying herbs. Heather, who is primarily in charge of navigation, has a large table for her charts, and I have a small desk of my own for our marine research. Our mission is to save humpback whales from poachers and help the endangered wildlife of the oceans. Both Heather and I have the power to call and to speak to the whales at will.

The sea whisks by the hull of our ship and, eventually, Heather gives the order to weigh anchor. Throwing an old cinder block tied to a string over the railing, we decide it is time to go explore and get supplies from the island where we have landed.

Picking up buckets and slinging them over our arms we make our way cautiously through Heather's backyard fence and look around. Hundreds of various food sources grow in the clumps of bushes and weedy growth at the edge of her yard, and we know from experience which ones will be the most useful. Both of us set to work harvesting. There are square-stemmed woody plants that, with their outside layer removed, reveal a soft reedy material that can be cut up into crab meat. There is also a plant with thick green leaves that, when dug out of the ground, has a bulby root system that can be peeled and chopped. We collect pinecones and red berries from shrubs for *jam. We also pick various leaves and dandelion stems. Finding a few more broken, hanging flower baskets and string we make our way back to the ship and climb aboard. It is a good thing, too, because the wind has begun to change, and it is going to be all we can do to miss the oncoming storm.*

While my creativity and enthusiasm flourished at home, at school I was increasingly caught in the middle between the two types of programs I needed. In math, the regular education classes were way over my head. In spite of my abilities in handling ideas and expressing myself, I was held back from enrichment programs, because my abysmal math test scores pulled down my overall rating.

As a result they continued to keep me in the mainstream classroom. But the standard curriculum didn't meet my needs at all. Following the regular education program not only robbed me of the support I desperately needed in math, it also prevented me from joining in the programs that would have stimulated my creativity and self-confidence — and would have afforded me the opportunity to spend time with other kids who also did not fit in the mainstream class.

Before entering fourth grade, I had taken a test to see if I would be eligible for the Talented and Gifted (TAG) program, designed for children believed to have exceptional abilities and who need an advanced curriculum. During the school day, the TAG students participated in an entirely different schedule from the rest of us. They arrived at school earlier in the morning, and they left school earlier in the afternoon. They had separate recess times, different field trips, a separate lunch hour, and an entirely different curriculum. Kids in the TAG program had separate art classes, music classes, gym classes. They watched different movies, listened to different class speakers, and were paired with mentors from the community to work on a specific area of interest — everything from architecture and law to visual art.

I did not make it into the TAG program. My test scores in math were not high enough. However, some of my good friends did. As students in the regular education program, we made fun of the students in TAG. We called them the Nerd Herd, but I knew that behind the words we were jealous. Looking back, I know now that my logical social group was the TAG students. But from the minute they entered those separate classrooms, the TAG kids formed strong social attachments that followed them all the way through junior high and high school — into band, orchestra, choir, and AP classes. I did, however, catch a glimpse into that world midway through my fourth-grade year. I was invited to join an Odyssey of the Mind (OM) team. At the time, Odyssey of the Mind was something that only the TAG program kids participated in, but there was a group that needed one more member to be eligible for competition.

Sunlight streams in through the tall gymnasium windows, casting cathedral-like streams of light into the dim, creaking cavern of the room. Steve and Ryan are actively engrossed in rigging together the electromagnetic wand they have designed. Crafted from PVC pipe, a car battery, wire, and a metal washer, it looks rough and homemade, but it will be effective. Megan and I have leaned the open refrigerator box up against the edge of the old stage at one side of the gym. Drop cloths are scattered below us, spattered in white specks from the base coat we have just used to cover the cardboard.

Our problem is entitled "Atlantis" and our mission is to work together as a team of seven to create a vehicle that can explore the ocean floor in search of artifacts from the lost city of Atlantis. Our vehicle cannot be pushed or pulled, and those operating the vehicle must remain inside it. The vehicle itself must stay inside a carefully measured square, and within that square several artifacts all made by us must be placed. Without using any hands, each artifact must be picked up and recovered by the vehicle and taken to a finishing point within a seven-minute time period. There also has to be an original story line accompanying all of this. Whichever team successfully recovers the most artifacts, in the most creative way and within the time period, will win the competition. The team with the highest score, when combined with the spontaneous problem solving score, will get to go on to the state championships.

Being the only member from outside the TAG program, I have to work extra hard to stay on top of things, since the other team members have all day in class to bounce things off one another. But I feel content here, whole — something I haven't felt in a long time. I feel like I do when I creatively play with my friends. I feel engrossed, like I have a sense of purpose, I am a part of something and am a real contributing member. I feel my brain firing on all levels, ideas soaring through it. We're really going to make this thing happen, really make this thing work and go.

I begin to make the downward strokes of black paint that will be the vertical lines of the white columns we have decided to depict as a part of an underwater scene. Megan begins work on a purple fish that swims long and huge between seaweed and pillars. We take a snack break. Mrs. Agostinelli cuts up apples and cheese and pours juice into paper cups, and we sit down at a foldout table. We talk about Greek culture, brainstorm ideas for a cover to the vehicle, and talk about things we need to work on for our spontaneous problem, which will involve creatively coming up with answers to a question in a short time period.

It's so wonderful to be part of a group like this where everyone is included, where everyone loves ideas and words and knows how to brainstorm. I wish I could spend the rest of my day here, sharing ideas, laughing, making plans.

I would have loved to stay with this OM group all day, every day. I liked these classmates, and I was excited by the ideas and all the things we could learn about. But that was not to be. Once the Odyssey time period was over, I returned to my regular daily rhythm, and they continued on with their TAG classes.

The next year, fifth grade, was a blur of barely passed or failed spelling tests, failed or missed math concepts, and struggles with grammar. I was placed along with three other students in a slower math group. We sat separately from the rest of the class and worked on review math while the rest of the class moved forward. However, no one knew just how really far behind I was. I had become such a master at masking and covering for what I didn't know that my teacher had no idea I couldn't tell time. My parents had engaged a tutor for me in fourth grade, and I had spent a great deal of time working with this very patient woman. However, two years later, I was still lost.

The only part of the day I hated as much as math was English. I hated pulling out the heavy textbook and opening it to a page, only to copy out sentence after sentence and then spend what felt like forever looking for predicates, nouns, verbs, or rewriting the sentences until they were correct. All of it was a huge jumble in my mind. I couldn't keep the rules of grammar straight and remember where commas, semicolons, or quotation marks should go.

Discovering Writing

I CONTINUED THROUGH

the highs and lows of school,

and then one day something

happened. That was the day

Mrs. Pratt used our "English"

period to have us write

descriptive paragraphs, and I

discovered the magic and power

of writing.

I am given a desk next to Mrs. Pratt's and the honor is not lost on me. Even though I hate English, she is my favorite teacher and I feel like we have a special rapport.

It is the English portion of the day, which usually means copying and correcting sentence after sentence. I am ready for the torture to begin. I pull my textbook out of my desk. I have my pencil ready and my piece of lined paper from the pile at the front of the room. "You will only need one piece of paper and a pencil today," Mrs. Pratt's voice announces over the mumble of the class. She walks over to her desk, picks up a stack of papers, and moves to the front of the room. "I am going to give each of you a picture of an animal I have torn from a magazine. You have to use the animal you get, no trading. I want you to look at your animal and write a paragraph describing what you see. Please keep all of the grammar we have talked about this year in mind as you write, and pay attention to the spelling, but don't be afraid to just get your ideas down on paper. We can fix up mistakes later."

She begins to move around the room, passing out pictures. Some students quietly accept their animal, some make sounds of disgust, others squeal with joy or hiss, "Yessss!" or "I love monkeys!" She stops by my desk and places a colorful photo in front of me. I can tell it has been torn out of a National Geographic. It is a picture of a painted turtle rising up out of the black water of a pond. He appears to be pulling himself up onto a protruding log. Thousands of bright green dots of algae float all around him on the water's surface. His neck is stretched to show his red-and-yellow stripes and the folds in his wrinkled army-green skin.

Mrs. Pratt finishes passing out pictures, and she places a tape in the tape player she keeps at her desk. A clicking sound follows as she pushes the PLAY button down. Flowing, quiet piano music fills the classroom. I look down and feel my hair fall forward across my cheeks as I begin to study the image of the turtle in front of me, eyes scanning the shades of bright and dark green, the reds and yellows, the black darkness of the water. I begin to imagine my pulse gradually slowing to the thudding cold-blooded pace of the turtle's heart. I feel my neck muscles tighten and imagine the stretch as he raises his head to the sun. How good sunlight would feel on his skin after a long winter. I try to feel his ancientness, a vast open space of time, the wisdom and knowing of ages. I sense the deep ache of loneliness and isolation he feels. I am reminded of something my father mentioned in the car the other day about the disappearance of wetlands due to development. With this thought I am overwhelmed by how powerless the turtle is. There is nothing he can do to stop things from changing, to stop time.

It is like talking when I begin to write in cursive along the blue lines of my paper. The images and ideas come quickly, no separate sentences or halting or faltering with verbs, subjects, or commas. Connected thoughts begin to flow. My hand forms the words. I incorporate the plaintive background music into the flow, every rise, every fall giving rhythm to the sentences. I didn't know that words could do this, that I could convey on paper the same process I used in my head to think about the world around me. Amazing! Writing was a way to communicate what my inner voice was saying. I hadn't ever made the connection that this was what writing was for.

I complete the last sentence and I feel empty, drained. I begin to open up again to my surroundings, and I realize how removed from the classroom I have been. First, I become aware of voices, then I become aware that I am sitting at a desk, a pencil in my hand, a piece of paper in front of me. I become aware of the fluorescent lighting, blue carpet, the students around me. Space and time meet up, but I can't tell how long I have been writing. Has it been minutes, hours? I look down and read what I put on the page.

As the morning sun slowly appears in the sky, life begins to stir in a pond long forgotten by the rest of the world. A gust of wind blows across the pond, causing ripples in the once-calm waters. Slowly, a creature pulls himself along a protruding log. With sadness in his eyes, he seems to be waiting for something that will take years to understand, but only a second to happen. This wondrous creature is the painted turtle. With his stripes of gold and red, he sits listening to the sounds of progress; they are distant but come closer every day. Soon this once-forgotten pond, full of life, will be destroyed as will many others of its kind. If we don't save the painted turtle and his world, who will? As the turtle quietly slips into the water, the sun begins to set and for just a moment silences progress.

I feel a warm glow, and I am excited about what I have created. I am ready to have Mrs. Pratt read my paragraph over for mistakes; I also want to find out what she thinks of it. I walk up to her desk, and my stomach flutters with anticipation. She smiles and takes the paper from me. I watch her face as she reads it. The look of pleased wonder causes me to flush with excitement and joy. She likes it, too. She thinks my writing is something *special. She even looks a bit surprised. She reads through the piece again, marking all of the spelling and grammar mistakes with her red pen. I don't care that it's covered with red. She likes my thoughts and ideas. I take the paragraph back to my desk to rewrite it with the corrections, feeling proud of what I have written.*

The discovery that writing was more than just spelling and grammar was a huge awakening for me. I realized that what I had to say and how I chose my words could be powerful. That if I didn't worry about the details anymore, and just focused on the words, how they sounded together and what ideas they conveyed, then I could produce writing with meaning.

Writing afforded me an ego boost as well. With each new piece, I eagerly gathered up the compliments from teachers and my parents, spurring me on to write more. I had pieces published in the *Friday Flyer* — a newsletter that went home to parents from my teacher — and I even had something published in a national magazine that published student work.

Over the next few months, my writing began to serve an even bigger purpose for me — it became my emotional outlet. I had begun to experience strong surges of melancholy during the past year or so, and now I was able to channel them into a form that allowed me to express them. Even when I was not feeling them directly, I tapped into the emotions. I would sit at our computer at home and let my feelings take over. In almost every piece I wrote there was a note of longing, of sadness, and of isolation. Sometimes I could even bring myself to the verge of tears as I sketched thoughts into my journal or worked on writing a descriptive paragraph.

In sixth grade, this discovery of writing was my lifeline. My writing gave me some sense of sanity amidst the increasingly difficult challenges I was facing to keep up in my other school classes. Despite my newfound joy in writing, I continued to feel anxious every day, especially in math class. I was withdrawing from friends and spending most of my time alone. Deep down, without even consciously thinking about it, I knew change was coming. I knew that things were not going to stay the same, and it terrified me.

A familiar knot in my stomach seemed to accompany me everywhere I went and the melancholy feelings grew stronger. The summer between fifth and sixth grade, my family had taken a trip to visit my grandfather who lived in Henrietta, New York. He lived in an old farmhouse built in the 1840s, complete with creaking, slanted doorways and sloping floors. One night during our stay, I woke up shaking with a horrible stomachache and panicky sense of fear and foreboding that overwhelmed me. I never actually threw up, but the discomfort and shaking didn't stop until I forced myself back to sleep. Initially, I wrote off the incident as some sort of weird bug. But the same thing happened again a couple of months later, and then again and again with even more frequency, until by the spring of sixth grade, the stomachaches were a daily part of my life. Growing concerned by my constant stomach complaints, my mom made an appointment with a pediatrician to see if he had any answers.

The waiting room of the pediatrician's office never changes. The same tattered stacks of magazines fill the neatly spaced end tables, a couple of children's books with a few pages inevitably colored or clumsily torn out, and two illustrated young people's editions of the Bible. Mom and I sit in the chairs against the windows. I do not want to be here, I never want to come to the doctor's.

My mom had insisted and coaxed, claiming that all the stomachaches I had been having were not normal, and we should get it checked out. Deep down, I had to admit that part of me hoped that they would find an answer. Nothing too serious, just an answer as to why my stomach bothered me all the time, why I would wake up in the middle of the night and not be able to fall back asleep.

A young mother walks in with one arm looped through the handle of a baby carrier, and the other grasping the small hand of a toddler. She sits down and lets go of the toddler, who immediately grabs hold of the nearby table to steady himself and knocks an entire pile of magazines to the floor with one awkward sweep of his arm. The basket of brightly colored toys catches his eye, and he staggers toward them and begins to play. Meanwhile, his mother lifts the baby from the carrier and holds her against her chest so that the baby's face is clearly visible over her mother's shoulder.

The round pudgy face, the eyes dark and clear, moist lips sucking in and out. Her little nose just two small holes and a bump of soft flesh. She sees me and a smile wide and slow illuminates her face causing her eyes to disappear behind raised mounds of flesh. The smile does not fade but instead she smiles wider, and wresting her hands free of her mom, begins to make clapping motions. Pure, unmitigated joy. A pang of lonely envy, of longing, shoots through me, a longing for something I felt once and lost. I look at the smiling face, and I think of all the years she has ahead of her —and of all the years I've left behind.

"Samantha," the nurse's voice calls out. My mom and I both stand up. I walk ahead, my mom follows. The nurse leads us to a scale where I step up and she reads my weight, and then we make our way down a long hallway to an examination room. I am asked to have a seat on the high table, my mom takes the chair. The whole room is plain except for the boarder strip of wallpaper trailing around the room with animals from Noah's Ark gaily marching into the boat over and over again. The nurse asks why we are here today, and Mom says it is because I have been experiencing chronic stomachaches. She asks a few more questions, some of me and some of my mom, and then asks us to wait for the doctor.

As the door to the room swings shut behind her, I make one last protest to my mom exclaiming that I still can't understand why we are here. She goes through it all over again and asks me some questions about school. A light knock, the door opens, the doctor walks in. A big smile on his bearded face, he shakes hands with my mom, then with me, and takes a seat on the wheeled stool beside the table. He begins to ask a battery of questions. When do the stomachaches usually occur? What kinds of foods have you eaten before they happen? He works his way through the usual routine checkup while he talks to us. He looks in my ears, nose, throat, listens to my heartbeat, has me take a few deep breaths while he listens through his stethoscope. He has me lie down and places his hands on my stomach to feel for any irregularities.

"Well," he says, allowing me to sit up. "You're perfectly healthy, nothing out of the ordinary. I'm going to say that you probably have some sort of mild lactose intolerance, so I would stay away from milk and dairy products for a while. I'm going to prescribe some Mylanta. Take a spoonful of it when needed for stomachaches." My mom asks a few more questions, then accepts the square piece of paper with his handwriting cast across it.

Well, maybe that's it. Maybe I am allergic to milk. Maybe that is the problem, maybe avoiding dairy products will make the stomachaches go away and the Mylanta might help. Deep down, however, I know it isn't this simple.

We leave the office and make our way out to the car. Mom tries to sound encouraging, but there is something beyond her words, in her eyes, her voice, that I know is sinking along with the sinking feeling in me. I know that deep down she knows this isn't the answer and so do I. As I climb into the passenger seat and pull my seat belt on, I feel myself pull in, fall silent, feel heavier than before.

THE NEXT FALL I STARTED

junior high school. I wasn't pre-

pared for the enormous changes

that would unmask my hidden

learning problems and inner tur-

moil. During seventh grade every-

thing fell apart. Since I was

five years old, I had been a stu-

dent at the same grade school.

For all of those seven years I had walked to school from my house that was kitty-corner from the front yard of the school. By the time I reached the sixth grade I knew just about every teacher there. I knew the librarian, the art teacher, the music teacher, the school secretary. I knew the principal, the janitor, the gym teacher, the cafeteria cooks and servers. I had grown up with the group of students who were my classmates. We were well aware of one another's strengths and weaknesses.

Despite my struggles, elementary school had become a completely familiar environment. There, I had been able to successfully string together webs of coping and compensation strategies that allowed me to mask what I could not do or did not know. I never had to tell time because we always moved as a class from event to event. When it was time to go to gym class we lined up at the door as a group, when it was time to go to art we did the same thing. All I had to do was watch the body language of the other kids to know when recess was about to begin or when the music class was ending. It didn't matter that I couldn't read a clock. I had found ways to maneuver through the system and still look like I knew what I was doing.

I had the same teacher for every subject, and it didn't take me long to figure out how to read each of them, how to get answers from them without them realizing it. They knew me, too, and they understood that I needed extra time or help on some assignments. They also knew my strengths: what I could do, what I could accomplish.

Leaving elementary school at the end of sixth grade meant that all the webs I had built for survival were going to be torn away, leaving me exposed. I would be forced to start from scratch, creating my safety nets all over again in an unfamiliar and much more complex environment.

Seventh grade was going to be full of new challenges. For the first time, I would have to ride a bus every morning to get to school. This meant that I would be assigned a bus number that I would have to keep track of. As September approached, I began to worry about not finding my bus, or missing the bus, and the humiliation that would bring. All this, despite reminders from my parents that I would know people on the bus, have friends I could look for, have bus attendants to ask, and that the bus pulled up in roughly the same spot every day. They didn't understand that I wanted to look like I knew what I was doing. I wanted to look like everyone else, who always looked like they knew what they were doing. I wanted, needed, to fit in. But I had the horrible feeling that I wouldn't, I couldn't.

Attending junior high meant that I would also have six or seven new teachers, one for each subject. None of them knew me. None of them had any idea that I struggled with math and grammar. None of them knew that I needed more time on homework and certain in-class assignments. I was also going to have two locker combinations to remember — my gym locker combination and my school locker combination. On top of all this, I was scheduled into a regular beginning algebra class, and I still didn't even understand basic addition and subtraction. The prospect was terrifying.

The week before school began, seventh-grade students and their families were invited to the school to pick up schedules and books, and to look around. My mom and I spent a couple days walking around the school, practicing every step. She helped me memorize where my classes would be because I was anxious that I wouldn't be able to find the room numbers. We also practiced opening my locker, working the combination over and over again.

I feel the ridges of the metal knob on the combination lock pressing into the pads of my index finger and thumb. Turning it slowly, I am focused on the little arrow and lining it up with the white 20. My entire field of vision, my entire being, is focused on that round lock. Matching the arrow with the 20, I pause, relax my muscles a little, feel my jaw loosen a bit, then tighten again as my finger and thumb clamp back down on the knob. I begin turning it back in the other direction. This time I am after the 9.

I reach the 9, pause again, get ready to spin the knob forward, but a sinking feeling makes my hand go limp and fall away. I feel a wave of disappointment, then frustration. The world around me fills in, the fluorescent lighting, the wide hallway opening up on both sides of me, the tall, skinny, pale-yellow metal locker, still sealed shut in front of me, one of hundreds of lockers that stretch the entire length of the hall.

"Did you get it?" My mom comes up behind me. She has a lift and lilt to her voice, a positive drive at pretending to hope for the best, even though we

both know that it isn't working. The positive voice is always her response to my negative one, but I hear something under this and know that she really does worry.

"No," I say, adding a little more dejection to my voice than I really feel. Hoping for even more sympathy from her, hoping to break her positive mask, hoping that if she finally admits it's hopeless, she'll just say, "Forget it!" and we can walk out together.

"Did you clear the lock first?"

"Yes."

"Did you turn it forward to the twenty?"

"Yes," I snap with impatience.

"OK . . . I'm just trying to help." Her voice remains calm with its persistent positive lift. "Did you go backward to the twelve?"

I let out a heavy breath, my eyes roll back, and I feel a thrill of anger, frustration, and helplessness rush through me. My voice comes out quieter than I expect. "I thought it was nine." My chest tightens with defeat. I hear her take a breath to help fortify her positive attitude. I notice my muscles tighten. I am ready to walk out. "I thought it was twenty, nine, twelve. This is the seventh time in a row I've done it wrong. I'm never going to be able to do this!" My face is hot, my eyebrows are raised. I feel like I am about to cry with these last words.

"OK . . ." The positive lilt wavers. "Show me what you did."

"I just told you I did twenty, to the . . ."

"OK, but, hon, I need you to show me so we can try it again." I pause and give her my "it's hopeless" look, then turn toward the locker. I pick up

the metal lock and hold it in one palm, while the other hand turns the knob.
I can feel my mom watching. She is leaning one shoulder up against the
locker next to mine. I start to focus in, spinning the arrow to the 20 and
stop. I pause, getting ready to move to the 12. I hear my mom say, "Good,"
under her breath. I feel encouraged. Then I freeze . . . blank . . . nothing. I
can't remember the number. I don't remember what's next.

"Come on, you know it." She has learned to say this with a supportive
tone, not a demanding one.

"I don't . . . I can't think of it. . . ." Tears well up again.

"It's nine, hon. Remember . . . nine."

I spin the arrow to the 9 and pull the round part of the lock down and
away from the loop of metal, take it from the handle of the door, then pull up
to open the locker.

It opened that time. But I wasn't at all relieved. No matter how
many times we practiced, it never seemed to stay with me. I wondered and worried about what would happen when I didn't have
time to mess up — when I couldn't rely on my mom for help. I
was terrified of being embarrassed and desperate to retain my
identity as a smart kid. Now I was even more worried. I definitely
was not looking forward to the first day of school.

My locker-opening ability continued to be haphazard at best
during the school year. I often packed the whole day's worth of
books and class work into my backpack, so I didn't need to open
my locker at all, and I could avoid the possible embarrassment of
not getting it open in time for class. My anxiety levels at the

beginning of seventh grade were already sky-high, and I felt like a phony. I believed that if anyone found out what I couldn't do or how hard basic things like opening my locker were for me, they would feel like I had been lying to them — they would wonder why I hadn't said anything up until now. They would think that I didn't belong. They would see the smart, wise, well-behaved, talented Sam for who she really was — a terrified, lost, inept girl.

Once junior high began, I faced another new challenge involving my familiar nemesis: time. I would now have six minutes between classes and it would be up to me alone to get myself to class on time. This was a problem because not only could I not read clocks, I lacked an internal sense of time. I didn't know what six minutes was or what it felt like, let alone how long it took me to get to my various classes spread out around campus. As a result, I lived in constant fear of being late for class.

Instead of socializing like other students did in the hallways between classes, hanging out in groups at lockers, walking together and waiting for one another, I was so anxious about being late for class that I would speed-walk to my locker, struggle to get it open, and then speed-walk to my next class. Sometimes I would even preplan my route in my head so I wouldn't lose any time. Often I was the first person in my classroom. I even remember getting to my classroom door and then stopping and ducking into a nearby bathroom and waiting there until I counted to sixty just to make it look like I wasn't such a Goody Two-shoes, eager to be early.

Adding fuel to my anxiety was the fact that I had been placed in a regular algebra class. In spite of my previous difficulties with math, I was expected to perform like everyone else. However, as the year progressed, it became apparent to my algebra teacher and the rest of my classmates that I wasn't like everyone else. I didn't understand. I couldn't be called on for answers. When we were asked to trade tests with a neighbor for correcting, I would blush and apologize, preparing whoever it was for just how many wrong answers I was likely to get. Sometimes, as an act of mercy, my teacher would take my paper and correct it himself. He worked hard to get me through from class to class.

Mr. Wilson clamps down on his toothpick and sends a hard gaze at the group of boys joking around in the back of the classroom. Most of the boys notice the unusual quiet, see Mr. Wilson, know he means business, and settle down. Mr. Wilson, his timing impeccable, waits until they are quiet and then barks out a coachy witticism that causes the whole group to break out into controlled laughter, lightening the mood, and restoring attention to Mr. Wilson, his wax pen, and the algebraic equations he taps out on the glass of his overhead projector.

I sit in my assigned seat up close to the projector and watch Mr. Wilson's thumbnail dig into the wrapping of his wax pencil and pull off another long curlicue shaving, revealing more of the tip. I am quiet and tight inside, writing down the examples from the board, copying the numbers as I see them — without any understanding of their meaning. Mr. Wilson taps out a new equation and in his matter-of-fact voice, spells out the logic of the next sequence of steps and numbers. He fields a few questions along the way. I watch attentively but my focus shifts in and out, my brain exhausted from trying to wrap itself around ideas that I cannot grasp.

He pauses as he finishes tapping out the last of the problem, removes the toothpick from his mouth, holds it out in the air with his left hand, and asks a question of the class. Hands shoot up all around me, a forest of arms straining and connected to minds that understand, to minds that know. I feel embarrassed confusion, not sure where to look or what I should do with my hands. I am the only one without my arm raised in the air. A slight tinge of shame flushes my cheeks. I feel anxious and exposed. This feeling has become as familiar as water. Every day the nervous flutter, the twinge inside, the blank, the sinking reminder that I don't get it, that I don't belong here, that I am alone.

Mr. Wilson finds his answer and then clears a space on the projector's surface and begins writing down the homework for the night: page 104, numbers 20–40, and page 106, numbers 1–24. He then assigns two pages of problems for us to solve. We are to use the rest of our time in class to begin work and ask questions. I know the routine. I open my book to the right pages, survey them for a moment so that it looks as if I am sincerely giving it a try. I find a new blank sheet of paper and carefully, slowly write my name, date, and class hour in the top right-hand corner, then hold my pencil poised so that it looks as if I am about to start tackling the problems, while with my other arm I raise my hand and wait for help to arrive.

Mr. Wilson makes his way up the rows, stopping off at various desks, leaving me for last because he always ends up kneeling beside my desk for most of the in-class work period in an attempt to help me. Eventually, I hear him come up behind me. He haltingly drops down to one, then the other knee. "Alright," he says, a playful scowl on his face as he wrests the pencil free of my hand, "let's see what you got." I smile at him and pull out the homework sheet from my math book, erased and re-erased time after time. I hand it to him.

There is an unspoken understanding between Mr. Wilson and me, formed over the weeks and months we have been working together. He knows that he is up against something he cannot conquer, something he cannot understand. He recognizes that no matter what either one of us does, I don't get it — and probably never will. I understand that despite this fact, he has to pretend that there is still hope, that I am still a viable member of this class. And I realize that I still have to attempt to complete the assignments and try my hardest to understand the material presented, even though we have moved so far beyond what I can comprehend that I am lost and buried.

He finishes looking over my homework, circling several problems and then, laying the paper back down in front of me, he begins to go over them pointing out what is wrong with each one and how to fix it. I am attentive and try to ask questions when I can formulate them. For flashes of time I understand a concept he explains or see it as he breaks it down, but the insight doesn't stay with me, and I often find myself unable to remember or do the process he just demonstrated a moment before.

We spend the rest of the class period working together. "Well," he says, realizing that, once again, despite both our best efforts I am not any further along, "don't worry about the in-class stuff and just focus on the homework *for tomorrow. If you want to come in early in the morning, we can sit down and go over it before class." I thank him and begin to pack up my bag, grateful that the class is almost over. He stands up and in his booming voice reminds the class about the upcoming test, but is cut off by the bell that releases us out into the hallway.*

Panic

WITHIN THE FIRST MONTH

of seventh grade, my stomach-

aches had become more intense

and more frequent. I grew terri-

fied of being sick. By November,

the episodes were happening sev-

eral times a day. I often sat in my

classroom wondering whether

this time I would get sick and

embarrass myself in front of

everyone.

I planned my escape route from the classroom, running through it again and again in my head, trying to map out each step.

Whenever a stomachache became believable enough, my anxiety mushroomed. I would begin to feel the room closing in. I felt trapped by all the faces, all the eyes. Self-conscious, I would start swallowing hard and would have to concentrate intently to focus on what the teacher was talking about. Sometimes, his or her voice would fade out altogether for minutes at a time as my own inner voice took over, loudly assessing my internal situation. Eventually, the attack would subside.

At lunchtime, I began to eat less and less. I would often skip breakfast at home because I invariably felt sick afterward, so I was usually starving by noon. However, I would only choke down about half of my sandwich and yogurt before I would begin to feel nauseated. Then I'd throw the rest of my lunch away.

It was at night, though, when the stomachaches and fear would really take over. It got to the point where I was so afraid of going to sleep that I would beg my parents to sit up with me and read or talk. At first they granted my requests and would stay for a little while, but I found myself always dreading their departure. Eventually they grew tired of my constant complaints of feeling sick and yet never actually getting sick. Their sympathy wore more and more thin until it took on a tough-love attitude of not wanting to feed into my irrational behavior. Eventually, they responded with outright frustration, and finally real worry, then silence.

I felt ashamed of my situation and angry at myself for acting this way, but I couldn't help the fear I felt — the persistent sense of dread. I would come home from school and want to fall to my knees and kiss the floorboards: I had made it through one more day! Then I would remember I had to go back again and the pit in my stomach returned. By bedtime the fear took over completely.

My room is on the second floor, and as I lie in bed, I listen to my dad's shifting weight as he walks through the house, my mother's muffled tones, the clinking of the dishes as Dad unloads the dishwasher, one of his habitual last tasks before bed. I hear the footsteps die away and the creaking swing of the back door opening as someone lets the dog out one last time. A few seconds later the door swings shut. My mother's voice has disappeared entirely, and I prepare for the final action of the night. My father walks from the back of the house to the front, pushes the front door closed, and turns the lock. Then his footsteps retreat and all is left in silence. Absolute unmovable silence.

My every muscle is tense, riveted to this world now void of sound. It is as if I can hear the breathing of every member of the house slow and become rhythmic, can feel their pulses ebb away. I know they are leaving me: Zac in his bedroom next to mine, my parents downstairs in their room at the back of the house. I can feel them retreat, sink deeper into sleep. My eyes explore the dark landscape of my room. The dusky forms of my dresser and chair, the mounds of clothing in my laundry basket are nothing but differing densities of black and shadow.

I notice a fullness in my stomach and I swallow hard. I purposely went to bed with an empty stomach, just to be sure. Or at least I thought I had. But now my stomach feels increasingly tight and sour. Underneath the even warmth of my down comforter my muscles are rubber bands ready to snap. I begin to swallow even harder and try to ignore the increasing sensations. This has happened night after night and I haven't once gotten sick, but every time I believe the feeling that I will. The stomachache does not go away. It's still there. I'm afraid I'll vomit.

My legs begin to shake. I sit up in bed, hoping that it will somehow make my stomach feel better. I hate this part — the waiting. I hate throwing up, choking, gagging like I'll never breathe again, the burning sensation. What if I don't make it to the bathroom in time? What if I can't wake my parents? I feel ashamed for wanting them, sheepish in having to wake them up. The trembling intensifies. My legs vibrate uncontrollably. Every muscle is on red alert for the final sign or signal that it is time.

I reach out toward the dresser next to my bed and flick on the light. The indistinct world that surrounded me instantly shifts into clear focus, full of recognizable objects. Adjusting my eyes, I swing both feet to the floor and decide to take action. My legs work enough to allow me to walk, but I can feel the muscles jerking and pulling, trying to spasm. Opening my bedroom door as quietly as possible, I pad across the dark TV room and into the little bathroom next to the stairs. I shut the door, anticipating all of its creaks and attempting to silence them. Then I flip on the light, reach for the faucet handle, turn on the cold water, and let it run.

I place my forefinger under the steady stream and take deep breaths, hoping to relieve the heaviness in my stomach. My fingers sense the water cooling until it's cold enough to send an ache up my arm. I cup my hands together and let them fill with liquid. Then, raising my hands to my mouth, I sip from them before all the water disappears through my fingers like a sieve. With each sip I pay attention to the cool water running down my throat, follow the cold feeling to my stomach, and pray that it finds emptiness. I envision the tight knot of my stomach forced to expand with the water's entrance, forced to loosen a little.

I turn off the water and the light and return to my room. I sit down again on my bed. The trembling continues while I prop up a third pillow on top of my usual two. I swing my contracting legs back up onto the bed and lean back against the pillows, pulling the comforter up around me. I reach over to my radio alarm clock and I switch it on, turning the volume down so that it is almost inaudible, an unrecognizable mumble of voices and music.

For an hour I sit there shaking. At times, the panic subsides and the trembling stops, then resumes again. Slowly, almost imperceptibly, my mind begins to shift to the voices on the radio. My mind begins to drift, comforted by the sounds of an outside world. I begin to forget my internal one. The lacerating knot in my stomach begins to loosen and give way to empty feelings of hunger and a small gurgle. My eyes begin to feel heavy, my breathing slackens, my legs ease and feel like immovable lead weights in their relaxed state. Eventually, inching my way down from my sitting position, I feel safe enough to turn out the light. All is very black for a few moments and then the dark shapes become visible again. I watch the sway of the trees outside until I drift off into unknowing.

As I became more anxious and fatigued with these night panics, I also became extremely self-critical. I always felt like I was ugly, fat, or out of style. I spent hours in front of the mirror trying to pick out clothes to wear. None of them ever seemed right and I would end up in tears crying and complaining to my mom. I was on a roller coaster emotionally. One look from a friend that I interpreted as critical, or an action I thought was a personal snub, would send me into a downward spiral of self-loathing and disgust. If I received a compliment or a good comment from a teacher, I would find myself on a short-lived high, but somehow I never felt like I owned the compliments I received.

My journal from this time is full of entries where I berate myself for not being smarter, or cooler, or better at having friends. Everything is my fault, my failing. Why else would I feel so alone even when I am spending time with friends? Why else would I be so afraid of things everyone else seems to take in stride?

Interestingly, I can remember that I continued to feel strangely superior as well. There are entries in my journal in which I remind myself that I am not like everyone else, that I am special, different, wise, unique — and that is why I always feel alone. I continue to feel like a heroine in my own story. And I tell myself that I was meant to be misunderstood, to be different, because I was meant for greater things. However, these words and ideas I used to comfort myself grew harder to hold on to.

As winter approached, my attacks of anxiety became increasingly worse and began to wreak havoc on the few friendships I had developed. I remember one time in particular at my friend Melissa's house when I got "sick" and had to go home.

* * *

Downstairs in the basement, under the metal tentacles of the old furnace, Melissa and I lie stretched out on an area rug. Our racing ideas, words, laughter, and the tape player we use to record the radio show we are producing totally absorb us. Melissa is Terry, the ditsy news anchor and weatherwoman. I am Ted, the pompously serious coanchor and reporter. Together we bring news, sports, and weather to our listening audience and go to commercial breaks that involve advertisements for places such as No Mercy Hospital — a state-of-the-art medical facility where one Kleenex will cost you only seven dollars. Eventually, we finish recording our radio show and race upstairs to play the tape for Marty, Melissa's mom.

We sit in Marty's prized ornate antique chairs, the ones we are not usually allowed to sit on, and listen, and laugh at the tape. I notice how different this upstairs room is from the basement. Up here, there are windows revealing that outside, the sky has dimmed into darkness and the yellow street lamps have come on. Up here, the TV flickers in the other room and the clock ticks, and there is furniture, and space and height and another whole floor above this one. I can feel myself shed the completely engrossing interior fantasy world my mind has been operating in, and become aware again of my place in reality. I begin to think about home. I am usually home by now. Then I remember. I'm not going home tonight. I agreed, hours ago, to stay the whole night. An unwelcome thought unfurls like a blanket shaken open over grass: Eventually, it will be bedtime, it will be quiet, dark, and I won't be going home, not tonight.

I block the thought out, try to realign my focus back to the tape, the laughing faces of Melissa and her mom. I successfully return to the present and go on listening and laughing, but this time I am not as whole-heartedly in the moment, this time my smile feels distant and hollow compared with the creeping sense of foreboding I can't shake off.

The tape ends and it is time for bed. Melissa's parents go upstairs first, and Melissa and I spend some time cleaning up the basement. Moving the bookshelf back into place against the wall. Picking up the scattered pages of our script. Eventually, we climb the stairs, turn off the light, and close the basement door behind us. My thoughts flicker again to ideas of home, a yearning to go back there. I notice I don't feel quite right. Nothing extremely wrong, nothing I would have noticed over the hum of activity tonight, but my stomach feels mildly funny. Not as empty as I had hoped — empty is comforting, a guarantee I won't get sick. No, instead my stomach feels full, a little cramped, but maybe this isn't new, maybe it has been this way for a while, since dinner, and I have been too distracted to notice.

We change into our pajamas and brush our teeth. Melissa cracks the door to her younger sister's room and slips in on a stealthy search for an extra pillow. My mind begins to race with excuses for why I can't stay. I say them out loud in my head only to have them all shot down as ridiculous by my own mind, and a pang of guilt strikes when I think about Melissa's disappointment if I leave. She climbs onto her bed and disappears under blankets. I open the sleeping bag spread out on the floor and lie down on it. Melissa reaches over and clicks off the bedside lamp. All is darkness.

We talk for a minute, reliving some of the best parts of the radio show, but I have a hard time staying interested in the conversation. The voice in my mind keeps talking louder as thought after thought surges, each one building on the last. I really don't think I feel well. What if I get sick?

I wish I could go home. *I feel my throat get dry and I swallow hard to stave off the impending queasiness, but it isn't easy. We say good night and Melissa rolls over onto her side.*

In the silent darkness, I try to close my eyes and just go to sleep. Just pretend that none of this is happening. I can hear the faint ticking of the grandfather clock downstairs, the muffled sounds of Melissa's parents' voices from their room. It's no use, the queasiness won't go away. What if I get sick? What will happen if I get sick? *My legs begin to shake, the muscles tensing and relaxing — even more of a sign that this is real, that I really am going to be sick: I feel a flash of heat and then cold.* What if I don't make it in time? *I just want to be home in my own bed in my own room. My stomach feels worse, acidic, aching.* I can't stand this anymore. *I debate.* Should I tell Melissa? Should I wake her up? What will she think? I can't do this to her again, what will she think?

The shaking gets worse and a wave of nausea passes through me. I swallow hard. I can't keep it in any longer, the feeling is too urgent, too intense. "Melissa," *I whisper.*

"Huh?" *a groggy voice in the dark.*

"I don't feel good. I think I am going to be sick."

"What?" *I hear the shuffle of covers. I swallow hard, and she reaches over to turn on the lamp beside her bed. Both of us squint in the light.* "Is it your stomach again?"

"Yeah, I'm sorry. I thought I was feeling fine. I might have to go home. Do you mind reading to me for a minute? Maybe that will help." *Melissa gladly pulls a book off of her shelf and begins to read.*

For fleeting shards of moments, the words, her voice, and the pictures distract me. But the ache is still there, the trembling continues, and my mind is consumed by the escalating feeling of dread, of panic. Waking Melissa up, having her read to me, just affirms even more that I will be sick. I hate bothering her for my sake, I hate asking this of her, I hate that she is seeing me like this. The feeling does not go away. I am still shivering. A wave passes through me again and I can't wait any longer. "Melissa, I think I'm going to have to go home."

Her response is sympathetic, and she offers to call for me. I insist on making the call. I go to the phone in the hallway and begin to dial my number. As it rings on the other end, my legs feel weak from shaking, but my head feels slightly clearer, a little more focused, my body a little more calm. I hear the phone pick up, my dad's quiet half-asleep voice answers. I respond in a voice sounding more feeble than I feel, and it startles me. I am surprised by how much work it takes for me to sound like someone who is sick, who needs to come home. My dad agrees to come get me. No questions asked this time, no second-guessing my request and decision. "I'll be there soon," he says. I feel a wave of relief and control, followed by another wave of shame and guilt as I place the phone onto its receiver and turn back to the bedroom where Melissa sits waiting on her bed.

I know Melissa is disappointed, and I know I have let her down. I know that she tries to convince herself that I am really sick, but deep down she doesn't think so. She could believe it the first time. It was coincidence the second time, but now, the third time, she wonders if my "sickness" only happens at her house. I would think the same thing if I were her, but I can't let *myself believe it. I must be sick, what else could it be? If I'm not sick, then something really must be wrong with me.*

I begin to pack up my stuff, and Melissa tries to be helpful. We walk down her stairs, my legs still shaking, then we wait in the dark to see the lights of my dad's car as he pulls up. The neighborhood is quiet and blanketed in snow. As we sit silently on the stairs, watching out the window, mixed feelings of guilt and relief move through me.

I see my dad's car as it edges up to the curb, snow swirling down the beams of light. I make my way to the door and apologize to Melissa. She says it's OK, but inside I know something is ending, that I have lost her trust in a way. I disappear out her back door and down the steps. I get in the car. It's warm. My dad looks sleepy, dressed in his coat and sock hat. He doesn't say much, and I quietly thank him for coming and try to explain some of my symptoms. He listens and murmurs a few words of sympathy. As we begin our drive down Sixth Street, I realize that Melissa may never invite me over again. But despite that knowledge and the guilt, my need to leave, to go home, and the relief I feel is stronger. The headlights of the car light up the falling snow and the stop signs ahead. I don't ever want to feel that way again. I don't want to spend the night at anyone's house ever again.

My Thirteenth Winter

MY FEAR OF GETTING SICK

began to take over and increas-

ingly get in the way. I could

sense my relationships crumb-

ling, and it felt entirely out

of my control to stop the

process.

It was like my life had become a movie and I was watching it fall apart, but I was powerless to do anything about it. I was no longer in control of the action.

Like all seventh graders I wanted to be liked and accepted. But my anxiety and my shame about that fear got in the way. Even when I was confronted about my isolating antisocial behavior, I was unable to admit the truth. I chose to lose friends rather than own up to my fears.

My friend Clare is considered pretty by everyone. She is blond and always seems to have a perfect tan. She styles her hair and spends time in the morning with makeup. Her clothes are always coordinated, along with a matching necklace or pair of earrings. She is nice to everyone, has a wide white smile, and blue eyes people are drawn to.

We have known each other for a while, played softball on the same team in the summer. We have a good time together talking about classes or mutual friends, but I know that I often make her uneasy, that she often wonders about me, can't understand why I am not happy at school, why I don't like going to parties, and avoid doing things. She understands me the least of all our friends, and this makes me feel lonely when I am with her and even more in need of her attention. I can't explain any of this to her. I can't explain my fears to her because she won't understand. She doesn't need to, she is living normally, doing all the things someone our age is supposed to.

We sit in her kitchen. She is eating carrots out of a Tupperware container, rolling them between her fingers with the polished nails, then snapping down on them with her white teeth. She leans in against the blue kitchen island, looks me in the face for a moment, and asks in a questioning but not unkind tone, "Why can't you ever just stay anywhere or spend the night?"

Even though I know she has been wondering it for months, her question takes me completely by surprise. I never expected someone to really ask me, to ever bring it up. Clare is the first friend to openly admit she noticed my strange behavior — and she is the least capable of understanding it. I know she and the others have wondered and talked about it amongst themselves. At times when I was with them I could read it in their looks. They were wondering why I always had excuses, why I didn't go to parties or dances, why I always went home without staying the night.

I open my mouth and take the necessary breath before speaking, buying myself a few seconds. Thoughts flash, my cheeks get warm, my eyes dart, and I feel my blood pulse faster. This could be my chance to finally give some explanation for my behavior. There is a rush of feeling, sensations that are nameless. I am unable to give them words, can't explain them. The answer is simple: I am afraid of throwing up and embarrassing myself. But how can I explain that to another thirteen-year-old? A thirteen-year-old who has never experienced anything like it in her life? How can I explain it to someone who sees the world so simply, so literally? How can I explain it to her when I don't even understand it or want to admit it to myself? I hope for an explanation that will satisfy us both, but all I can say is "I just can't. . . . I . . ."

Clare looks at me and I read confusion, frustration, and disappointment behind her slight smile. She has given me a chance, perhaps my last chance, to come clean. I can feel it. She tries to move on like nothing has *happened, seals the lid of the carrot container, and takes her time putting it away. In seventh grade, false feelings and false faces are the rule. To lose self-control would make you too vulnerable. Clare isn't satisfied, but she isn't going to say any more.*

My gaze returns to the windows where I can see the house lights come on across the lake, golden shining orbs along the dark band of shadows. I hear the sound of tires crunching on snow and turn my head to see the bright flash of headlights as my mom pulls into the driveway to pick me up. When I look at Clare to say good-bye, I know that something has changed. The gap between us has grown. I leave quickly, catapulting myself out to the waiting car, away from the awkward look and silence. Mom backs out of the driveway just as it begins to snow.

As the weeks pass, I hear less and less from Clare. I find out about parties and sleepovers after they have happened. I feel frustrated with myself, angry, isolated, but I also can't help but feel a sense of relief that I haven't been included. "It's actually a good thing," I tell myself. "I no longer have to think of excuses for why I can't do something or why I have to leave early. I would rather not have any friends at all than risk getting sick and losing control in front of them."

On all fronts I feel alone. My family doesn't understand what's wrong or why I do the things I do. Out of a yearning to help, they only make me feel more isolated, more like a misfit, more like I should be able to control myself. My friends know only the surface me, or at least that is how it seems, since that's all I ever show them. I am excluded — and even more often I exclude myself.

Looking back over my seventh-grade year, I can see the fear and anxiety attacks gradually chipping away at my world. However, at the time, it seemed very sudden, as if I woke up one morning and my world had become very small — I wasn't in control anymore. My fear became a separate force that could act at will. I was at its mercy. It was in control of me.

I stand in the bathroom getting ready for school. The sink faucet hisses as the water rushes from it, and the old floorboards creak beneath my feet. Above the sink is a mirror, a large one that stretches across the upper half of the wall and reflects the entire room. For the first time in a long time, I stand facing that mirror and really look at myself, or at least at the person staring back. I look at the gray skin and dark circles around the eyes, at the face that seems utterly small and slight. How easy it is to look past this face altogether, dwarfed by everything, the towel cabinet, shower curtain, laundry hamper. I am so easily made invisible; it is as if I've become a passing ghost.

It's been weeks since I've slept through the night, or been able to fall asleep after the light is turned out. My stomach troubles are an almost nightly occurrence now, keeping me awake for hours at a time. Morning always comes too quickly for me. Yet the feelings of panic and anxiety are not reserved for the dark and my bedroom; now they accompany me everywhere, all the time. My life has become regulated by these unpredictable moods. I don't undertake anything without a feeling of complete dread at losing control or getting sick.

My muscles are constantly tense. My stomach is habitually tied in knots. A milky film covers my world. Everything takes extra effort to accomplish, as if I am moving through water. I feel as if I am always walking on eggshells, carefully regulating all of my actions, all of my words, desperately trying to keep myself from making a mistake, from losing control.

I have completely given up on sleepovers and most other social activities. I will still go to a friend's house for a couple of hours, but with great effort and reservation, and with a set time I know I will be going home. I refuse to attend parties, won't go to dances. Every invitation seems like just another opportunity to get sick and embarrass myself. It's a burden, always having to invent elaborate excuses for why I can't do this or that. Even my parents have become desperate, worrying about my antisocial tendencies. They encourage me to stay out as late as I want, and they wear exaggerated looks of excitement on their faces when I get invited somewhere. I feel guilty when I tell them why I can't or don't want to go. They see through my excuses.

My dad can't relate at all to my aversion to social activities and becomes visibly frustrated with me. How can he understand? He was class president in high school and captain of the football team. He never has trouble being social and confident. My mom tries to be more patient, but eventually grows tired of my behavior as well, and we begin to have real battles over my lack of social interest. I know it is because they love me and want me to be happy that they worry about me and push me, but the pushing only leaves me feeling more inadequate and angry with myself. No matter what I do, I can't make these anxious feelings go away, I can't make myself feel comfortable in social gatherings or make myself look forward to them. I can't fix how out of place I feel, how much I feel I am being judged and watched. How terrified I am of saying or doing the wrong thing.

Simply going to movies or being in other public places is stressful as well. All I can do is dwell on the possibility of getting sick. I sit in a movie and have mini anxiety attacks, obsessing over whether or not I can get out in time, and how embarrassing it would be if I don't. It's as if this constant shadow is hovering around me, following me, demanding that it be reckoned with, that it be taken into consideration at all costs.

In school, this shadow is always present. I constantly feel sick. It is like I am running an obstacle course, avoiding mess-ups and mistakes all day long. I'm always relieved when the day finally ends, when the bus drops me off and I am home. But the tension never fully leaves me, the shadow doesn't disappear. It stays with me, controlling me. In fact, even now in the mirror I can see the shadow in my eyes. I feel so tired, so heavy.

Eventually, I turn the water off. Run a brush through my hair one more time. Turn out the lights. I walk out of the bathroom and into the hallway. My mom sits up in bed with the blankets pulled up over her knees watching the Today show. I know she worries about me even though she tries to keep it from me. I know she cries about me a lot. "Good morning," she offers brightly. "Are you off? Have you had breakfast? Did you eat anything this morning?" Her look is pensive, anxious, as she looks me in the eye and waits for my response.

*　*　*

At first, my parents had been frustrated by the constant stomach complaints, by my anxiety at leaving the house alone to help run errands, and the turned-down invitations from friends. They were tired of phone calls to come get me in the middle of the night, only to get me home and never experience me actually getting sick. However, with time, they couldn't help but notice my hollow, haunted look, the weight loss, the fact that I barely touched the food on my plate, the phone calls from school to come home early during the day because I wasn't feeling well. Finally, one night in early March it reached the breaking point.

Mom has made soup. She is constantly encouraging me to eat now. Everyone, including my brother, Zac, watches me anxiously. My mom has an all too sweet lift to her voice. Dad acts like everything is fine. The steaming bowl is placed in front of me: noodles, chicken, and celery floating in a yellow broth. A hunk of bread passed, crackers offered. I pick up my spoon, which feels heavy in my hand, and I dip it into the bowl, lifting out a steaming scoop and carry it to my mouth. It goes in, I swallow, moving the food around in my mouth to accommodate for the heat.

Zac and Dad begin a conversation, and Mom takes her place at the table. I eat another bite, and then, just as I lift the third bite to my mouth, my stomach tenses. I don't feel good and I can't eat any more. I push the bowl away and offer its contents to anyone who wants them. "I'm done," I say.

"Come on, hon, eat just a little more," my mom pleads, a worried expression clenching her face.

"I can't. I am not feeling well," I say.

My mom looks at my father for support and he repeats her plea in a forced, carefree voice, hoping this will entice me. Mom gets up from the table and walks into the kitchen. Zac looks at me. An expression I don't ever remember seeing before spreads across his face, a sincere look of concern. He suddenly looks very mature. "Sam, Mom is really worried about you not eating, you know. She cries about it a lot when you aren't around. You need to start eating more. You aren't eating enough. You're driving everyone crazy."

I feel like I have been kicked in the gut as I think about how much I am making everyone worry about me. Hearing it come from my younger brother's lips makes it feel even more serious. "I know," I say as I stand up from the table. "I just don't feel good." And I disappear upstairs to my room.

Later that night, my parents ask me to go on a walk with them. It is a dark night, no moon. The neighborhood lights are yellow and the black pavement shines with watery snow that has melted during the brief thaw. Our dog, Kelly, comes along, and gently my parents begin to tell me they are worried about me. They mention the weight loss, my refusal to eat, the stomach troubles, the tears. They ask me if I can explain to them what's wrong. I can't. "I just get stomachaches," I say. "I wish I knew why, I wish I could stop them, but I can't."

They tell me they are going to make an appointment for me to see someone, a psychologist who Dad knows and respects. I tell them I am fine, that I don't want to go. I outwardly protest, but inside I am too tired to fight them and I know I am desperate for something to change.

Not long after our conversation, I was called to the seventh-grade principal's office and given a note saying my mom had phoned and would be picking me up early from school. I felt relieved at the idea that I wouldn't have to spend the entire day at school but I also knew why I was being picked up early — it was because my parents had gotten me an appointment with the psychologist. I was both relieved and disquieted at the idea of having to talk to someone about my problems. She was another adult, and I desperately needed to portray myself as normal, competent, and creative to other people, especially adults whom I wanted to like and respect me. How was I supposed to tell her what was really happening or going on? She might think I was crazy.

I sit in the pale-green room with its shades half pulled and say nothing. I try to see beyond her to the titles of the books that fill the built-in shelving. Her voice is like the lighting, low and soft.

She wants me to describe my idea of the perfect place. My mind works to avoid any honesty. I want to please her, impress her, be what she wants so she won't see the real me. Not that I even know what my idea of the perfect place is. Instead, I tell her something she would want to hear: I tell her about an island, mention something about water and warm sun. It's the best I can manage without revealing anything about myself.

She asks me to close my eyes and I do. "Now," she says, "try to visualize your island in your mind." She pauses. "Do you see it?" I nod. "OK, I want you to let the feeling of the place take over, the warmth of the sun all around you, the calm, open water surrounding the shore."

My eyes are closed, but all I really see is darkness. I am still back on her first question trying to come up with my perfect place. I am bewildered by the idea. Whenever I start to get nervous, whenever I feel my stomach begin to ache, she wants me to stop my thoughts and go to my island? She says it will take practice and after a while it will happen naturally. Pretty soon the image might even help replace the fear I so often feel and prevent it from snowballing out of control.

I find myself nodding in agreement with her. I give promises that I will practice. But I feel overwhelmed with disappointment. This is it? I thought maybe she would have an answer that finally would make these attacks just go away. But she wants me to envision an island and my perfect place isn't an island. I don't have a perfect place — real or imaginary. How can she know what the true problem is? I haven't been fully honest with her. I don't believe I can be.

She isn't there when this thing — this panic attack as she calls it — takes over. She hasn't felt the paralyzing force of it. I can't really describe it to her or to anyone — the overwhelming hold it has on every breath I take, every movement, every thought. She doesn't know how dark, how deep this thing lives in me. How ashamed I am to admit its power over me. She doesn't know and neither do my parents, who eagerly enter the room at her request to hear her solution of mind travel to this island oasis. My parents, who desperately seek hope and relief for me in the idea of calm water and soothing sunshine, feel it is a wonderful concept and thank her for the week's session. We leave, the three of us; my parents are hopeful, while I have never felt more lost.

Winter has stayed longer than usual this year. We begin the drive back home. I want so desperately for someone to understand. I want to have the capability, the words to describe my anguish. I press my hand against the glass of the car window. It feels instantly wet, instantly cold. I hold my hand there for a moment, then decide to sweep downward, clearing a swath in the condensation, making a portal to the world we are passing. The snow is shifting down in horizontal lines and the darkness of the winter afternoon is closing in. The car sounds are muffled in the snow. We pass field after field, each one so empty, so alone. My mind is riveted to those fields that stretch away, wide open to the gray line of bare trees at their edges. I feel like those fields, filling up with snow in early darkness. How I want to just disappear into them, to drift off into the trees and be lost. I am so tired — every inch of me heavy and exhausted.

A Collaboration

AT THE END OF MY

seventh-grade year I was col-

lapsing on the inside. Luckily,

my seventh-grade writing class

became my life preserver. It was

the one thing that got me

through the anxiety and fear that

plagued me. No matter what I

couldn't do, I could write.

I found an identity in that skill and clung to it. I told myself again and again that I was special, that I was different and my ability to write was proof.

Mrs. Williams, my seventh-grade writing teacher, was instrumental in making her class a place where I could grow. It was her attention and her willingness to overlook my spelling and grammar mistakes for the real content and ideas in my writing that made a lasting difference for me. Here was evidence that I was important — that I had value. Hearing this from an adult other than my parents was extremely significant to me. Especially at a time when I could hardly face getting out of bed and going to school.

"Sam, you're a poet. You just don't realize it. Watch and I'll show you." Mrs. Williams picks up her red felt-tip pen and begins to make slash lines at what seem like random points in the sentences of the descriptive paragraph I handed her. "There," she says, finishing. "Now go rewrite this and begin a new line wherever I have made a mark. Then bring it back and we'll look it over together."

I return to my desk and pull out a blank sheet of lined paper from my notebook. I begin to do as she asked, rewriting the paragraph line by line, until my words form a narrow column down the page. I'm sure I hate poetry — at least I can't ever see myself writing it. All of it seems obscure and difficult to understand, or smarmy and all about love, and it all seems to rhyme. I can't imagine writing poetry — I mean, really writing it. However, Mrs. Williams thinks I can, that I already do, and she can't be wrong, not about something like this. But I'm still not convinced.

English is my favorite class of the day. All day I look forward to the challenge. I don't just pass or eke by here. I excell. I rarely feel anxious or inadequate, except perhaps socially. Here, there aren't any numbers; here, my teacher has a soft-spoken voice, rich with feeling, sincere. She listens, and she believes that I have a special gift with words.

I am quiet in class. Rarely do I share or speak at all unless it is to answer a direct question, or during one-on-one time with Mrs. Williams or another student. But she meets me halfway. Here, my individuality is validated. Here, other students admire my abilities, even though I am still quiet and studious and keep to myself.

The column of words is complete and I take it uncertainly up to Mrs. Williams's desk. She reads it quietly out loud. "This is a poem, Sam."

I smile despite myself, pleased, proud, but still disbelieving. "Really? You mean everything I have been doing so far can be turned into a poem just by changing the way it looks on the page?"

"Not everything. But sections or paragraphs where you use imagery to describe scenes or thoughts and feelings — that can be poetry."

I let this new revelation wash over me, sink in. Poetry doesn't have to rhyme? It doesn't have to be about love or anything like it? Poetry is a concise way to express feelings or describe the world around you? I am surprised by the idea. I reluctantly believe her — what I write is poetry already.

Even though Mrs. Williams's support was invaluable, I was still a seventh grader, deeply in trouble. I continued seeing the therapist and Mom eagerly encouraged me to practice her techniques, but no matter how hard I tried no island ever appeared. Session after session, I worked to elude her, to keep her thinking that I was a creative, smart, funny child. I wanted her to like me. Of course, I didn't really know what was wrong. She had given me a name to call my episodes of anxiety: panic attacks. But why they happened never became clear. In fact, the failure of this counseling experience left me feeling more hopeless than before. The panic attacks continued and anxiety still ruled my life. However, to my parents and counselor, I pretended that there was some improvement. I didn't want them to think that all their hard work was in vain. I knew how badly they wanted me to get better.

The difficulty with math and grammar continued. My parents bore witness to my struggles to complete math homework or correct grammar and spelling in my written pieces. Worried and concerned, they requested to have me evaluated again for a possible learning disability or to determine if I was at least two years delayed in my understanding of math — so that I might qualify for special services through the school.

The school resisted, citing my high grades in social studies and English classes and my average grades in science. They pointed out that I wasn't a behavior problem; in fact, I appeared to be well respected by my peers and was well liked by my teachers. I often went above and beyond in my completion of class projects and attended and showed aptitude in my choir, art, and home economics classes. They couldn't understand how a "good student" like me could possibly qualify for special education services. Nevertheless, they finally agreed to test me again.

I was tested in March of my seventh-grade year. The questions on this standardized Key Math test ranged from how many nostrils I had to how many quarts were in a gallon. The outcome was confusing. The evaluator's findings stated that my ability to "process and manipulate mathematical operations and concepts was at mastery level." However, according to the test, there were sixteen basic math skills that I had not yet mastered:

1. Determining two- and three-digit numbers depicted by visual representation of sets in hundreds, tens, and ones.

2. Determination of decimal tenths depicted by visual representation of a whole separated into ten equal parts.

3. Determination of a multipart fraction depicted in a set of up to ten objects.

4. Give the next number in a sequence of decimal values with equal increments.

5. Express decimal hundredths as a fraction.

6. Order decimal values from smallest to largest.

7. Identify angles of the same size within a set of angles.

8. Mentally add two-digit numbers using compensating strategies.

9. Mentally subtract from hundreds using compensating strategies.

10. Mentally multiply with 100 as the factor.

11. Determine the value of a set of coins.

12. Read a monthly calendar to identify the date at the end of a given interval.

13. Identify a unit of time that would be best to measure a given activity.

14. Identify a set of like coins that would equal a value up to five dollars.

15. Estimate the length of an object (1–12 inches).

16. Estimate the total cost of multiples of a given item whose cost cannot be easily multiplied.

In the Summary and Recommendations section following this list of unmastered skills, the evaluator stated: "Samantha's ability to perform in the regular math class is sufficient when given support. Several areas need to be developed further to assist Samantha with compensation skills." The evaluator suggested that the school "Provide repeated practice sessions with focus on using compensating strategies rather than learning new material."

These results were puzzling and contradictory. First, how could I be considered to have a mastery-level understanding of math when I had not mastered sixteen fundamental objectives on the test? Many of these skills, such as having a sense of the value of coins or being able to estimate the length of an object, are basic stepping-stones in the understanding of math. Virtually all of these unmastered skills would be necessary to perform the tasks required to succeed in a regular algebra class — the same algebra class I was currently failing.

Second, how could I stay in my algebra class, as the summary suggested, and yet do as the results also recommended — practice using compensating strategies on the old material rather than learn new material? How could I be expected to participate in a regular math class, ignore the new material being presented, and instead spend my time reviewing techniques so I could learn the concepts I was supposed to be ignoring?

Over the years, my parents had done everything the school had suggested. They had secured outside tutoring, worked with me at home. They even had my eyes tested and bought me glasses in third grade, when it was determined that I had a slight problem with fine motor skills. No matter how hard I worked or how often I sought help, I was failing my algebra class. The conflicting results and interpretations by the professionals of the Key Math test broke whatever little faith my parents still had in the system. They realized that they were going to have to take matters into their own hands to get me the help that I needed.

As the end of the year approached, my mom was desperate to find some constructive project that would counterbalance my dismal learning experiences at school. She recognized the importance that both writing and my relationship with Mrs. Williams played in keeping me going and encouraging what little self-esteem I had. My mom approached Mrs. Williams and asked if she would be willing to work with me over the summer. Mrs. Williams agreed and proposed that I meet with her weekly to work on writing poetry. She would give me assignments and guidance as well as help edit the pieces I wrote. I was a bit daunted but flattered by the idea that she was willing to work with me.

My mom and Mrs. Williams agreed that the work we did together would need some kind of focus. Aware of how I often used pictures or images to stimulate my creative writing, my mom wondered whether her longtime friend Charlie Murphy, a watercolor painter, might be persuaded to join in the project. Charlie had watched me grow up and my mom had shared some of my writings with him. He also knew about my struggles in school and wanted to help. Mrs. Williams had been collecting his paintings for years. Charlie agreed to loan me some of his images with the hope that I could write about them. Someone even suggested that if the process went well, and the writing and art matched, perhaps we would turn the collaboration into a book. A few days later, Charlie dropped off the first painting.

Pulled from its cardboard-and-garbage-bag wrapping, the painting Charlie dropped off leans against the edge of my bed, facing out. I have been drawn to this piece ever since I saw it on a gallery wall a year ago. I was instantly arrested by its design, colors, and the figure it portrayed — an old man who stood saying so much, feeling so much. Now, here it is, mine for a little while. I feel a strong connection to it, a pull. I sit down cross-legged on my bedroom floor in front of the framed image, open my journal to a blank page, put a tape into my stereo, and press PLAY.

The music fills the room in soft currents of sound. The figure in the painting is a man, old and balding, with a ring of white hair running around the edges of his head, continuing down into a white beard and mustache. He stands with his arms outstretched, head bent downward and slightly tilted, in an expression of quiet surrender, a relinquishing grace. His arms are held out away from him and he is draped in a kimono-like robe, its sleeves extending downward, its material patterned in bare trees, November branches in russets, greens, lavender-purples, auburns, yellows, golds, oranges, reds. His fingers tug or pull at long auburn ties, as if he is in the process of disrobing, shedding his cloak. The line of his extended arms and shoulders reflect the line of rounded hills behind him, and he appears to be fading into the landscape, disappearing into the tree line.

The feelings come washing over me in waves. I feel his age, his vast years of wisdom. I feel his loneliness in this last task he has to perform, those bare trees stretching on in the quiet cold late fall, winter oncoming in the wind. I feel myself ache. I feel my arms outstretched, weighed down by the heaviness of fabric and years, my hands gracefully, elegantly pulling the ties to release the robe, to let it fall away — because it is time, and I am tired, and I am at peace. I want to let go, I want to fade into the background. I hear his voice, know his thoughts, what he feels, I begin to write.

> I am old, the sun has set,
> it is time for me to fade into the background of life;
> Death has given me his cloak to wear.
> Do not worry, for his cloak is warm, and the chill north
> wind can no longer harm me.

I can feel my soul as it is pulled from me and
taken to a place where it can be at
peace forever.
It is time. My breath becomes the falling
breeze, and my body the solid
stem; my arms become the branches
reaching to a higher grace, and my
hair unfolds into leaves of light.
I have entered the forest of
eternity and stand as a tree should.
A sigh passes from my lips,
and all is still.
I am old,
and the sun
has set.

With these last words, I feel released and I come falling back into my-self. There is nothing more to say or feel. Disoriented, light-headed and tired, I get up.

I go downstairs to look for Mom, at work in the basement. I want her feedback. She's talking on the phone. I wait for some form of acknowledg-ment, and then wave the penciled poem, jotted on a blank page in my jour-nal. She seems a bit surprised and places her hand over the receiver. "But you've been gone for such a short time."

I shrug my shoulders, not sure what that means, or why it matters. She asks her friend if she can call her back and hangs up the phone. I give her the journal, return to my room, and wait.

It doesn't take her long. I hear her voice calling me, and I go back down. She gives me a hug and says it's wonderful and that she can't believe that I wrote such a beautiful piece so quickly. She has a look of wonder and pride on her face, and I feel a warm thrill at what I have created. She corrects a few things in light pencil, some of my spelling mistakes, and says that she can't wait for me to show Charlie and Mrs. Williams. I walk upstairs, journal in hand, flushed with pleasure and satisfaction. I look at the painting one last time before I wrap it up, perceiving my words in the old man's expression.

An Answer

WHILE I CONTINUED WRIT-

ing poetry evoked by Charlie's

paintings and worked with Mrs.

Williams that summer, a second

source of help arrived. My mom

discovered an organization called

the Learning Disabilities Assoc-

iation (LDA) of Michigan. We

started getting their newsletter

Outlook. One of the articles in the 1992 July/August newsletter was entitled "Gifted but Learning Disabled: A Puzzling Paradox" written by Dr. Susan Baum. In the article, Dr. Baum explains how students can be both incredibly gifted and incredibly disabled. At one point in the article she describes this type of student and explains how they typically go unidentified as learning disabled:

The second group of youngsters in which this combination of learning behaviors may be found are those who are not noticed at all. These students are struggling to stay at grade level. Their superior intellectual ability is working overtime to help compensate for weaknesses caused by an undiagnosed learning disability. In essence, their gift masks the disability and the disability masks the gift. These students are often difficult to find because they do not flag the need for attention by exceptional behavior. Their hidden talents and abilities may emerge in specific content areas or may be stimulated by a classroom teacher who uses a creative approach to learning. The disability is frequently discovered in college or adulthood, when the student happens to read about dyslexia or hears peers describe their learning difficulties.

As she read this article, my mom knew at once that she was reading about me. It was as if the author had been following me around, describing my life, my struggles! Mom recognized all of the pieces, the whole picture of my intellectual ability fooling everyone, overshadowing what I couldn't do, my disability. Other people — experts — had recognized this phenomenon. She wasn't alone; she wasn't crazy in believing there was something wrong, something out of my control. For the first time, my mom could give my problem a name: gifted and learning disabled.

After reading this article, Mom was convinced that I should not be expected to slog my way, failing, through another regular education algebra class like the one I was scheduled to attend in the fall. She knew that something had to be done. Armed with this article and determined to be heard, she set out to get what I needed from the school system.

My mom first approached my school guidance counselor Mr. Olson to see if there was any way I could be removed from the scheduled eighth-grade algebra class and be placed in special education math. Mr. Olson said he was sorry, but my test scores were not low enough. With the way the system was set up, I would have to fail more before they could look into getting me help. My mom was appalled by the idea that in an institution set up to help children learn and succeed, I was going to have to fail more before I could get the help I so desperately needed. Waiting, subjecting me to further failure, only meant more months of starvation, stomachaches, missed opportunities, and the further decay or complete destruction of what little self-esteem I still had left. This wasn't an option. She knew that they were already losing me.

My mom went directly from the guidance counselor's office to see the administrator in charge of special education, who, in previous years, had been reluctant to do anything with my case, until my test scores showed otherwise. She walked into his office, planted herself in a chair facing his desk, and announced that she wasn't leaving until she got some help and some answers — letting me continue to fail more first was not an option.

Unable to defend the idea that I should have to fail more math classes before anything could be done and confronted by my mother's absolute determination, the Superintendent of Special Education finally came up with a different way to evaluate me. He suggested that I be tested by grade-level objective to see if I knew the material I was supposed to know at the end of each grade level. The results of this test would help determine where my skills really were and just how delayed I was, if at all.

Ever since my mom had read the Susan Baum article and shared its content with me, I did feel a small sense of relief. What was wrong with me might actually be a real thing that other people could have, too! Maybe I wasn't crazy. If I had a learning disability or LD, it wasn't something I was doing wrong, it wasn't my fault. Instead, it was something out of my control, something I couldn't blame myself for. I found myself anxiously wondering what the test would show, anxiously waiting, hoping there would be evidence that my problem was real.

The test administrator and I sat in a high-ceilinged room in the school administration building for a couple of days. We began with a first-grade math workbook and worked our way up through the grade levels. The test results showed that I was ignorant of basic concepts from first through third grade, and that by fourth grade my understanding of math completely fell apart. Actually, she stopped the test at the fourth-grade level, acknowledging that there was no reason to go any further.

According to this grade-level objective test, I had not even come close to reaching a fourth-grade understanding of math, and was far more than two years delayed when compared with other eighth-grade students. This meant that I did, indeed, qualify for special supportive services and accommodations from the school.

We had found an answer to what had been wrong all these years. But there was still one more hurdle to jump over — getting the school to cooperate. Because of these latest test scores, my parents were finally able to get the serious attention of the school. A meeting was set up for the first week of my eighth-grade year to develop an IEP (Independent Educational Plan) to meet my special needs. Key staff and faculty attended, along with my parents and guidance counselor.

In this meeting, the test results were reviewed and recommendations were made on which services would be provided for me by the school. Mr. Wilson, my seventh-grade math teacher, who had worked so hard with me to little avail, reported on my performance in his class the previous year. He said that he had never seen anyone work so hard and fail so much. He also admitted that my final grade was based on my effort, not on my actual test and homework scores; he gave me a C+ as a final grade.

Several individuals felt very strongly that I should not be placed in a special education math class and that I should not be labeled as learning disabled. Some felt that my parents were overreacting and believed that they, particularly my mother, were the problem. They accused my mom and dad of being overprotective, and they proposed that my parents were the ones who put the idea in my head that I couldn't do math. They suggested that was the reason I performed so poorly.

Several in the meeting pointed to my overall high grades and achievements in other subjects and claimed that labeling me as a special needs student and granting me special services was unjustified. At one point during the meeting, a special education teacher leaned across the table and said to my mother, "Do you have any idea what you will be doing to your daughter by placing her in a room with those kinds of kids?"

My mom felt intimidated, frustrated, and was close to tears as the meeting drew to a close. The atmosphere was tense and divided. My guidance counselor, who had remained quiet throughout the meeting, now chose to speak. Calmly and concisely, Mr. Olson reminded everyone of my grade-level testing results, which, according to the school's standards, qualified me for special services. He reminded them of my struggles and noted that even though Mr. Wilson had not failed me, his evaluation was based on my work ethic, not on my comprehension of the material. As my counselor, he made a personal appeal, sharing his belief that getting me help via special education math was the right thing to do.

Mr. Olson's well-timed, cogent analysis prevailed, and the necessary papers were signed. However, several individuals left the meeting feeling that I was being done a disservice and that the system was being abused.

My mom came home that afternoon shaken and angry at the things she and my dad had been accused of, but also happy that I had finally qualified for special services. They had won. But she was also worried and could hear the woman's voice in her head saying, *Do you have any idea what you will be doing to your daughter by placing her in a room with those kinds of kids?* My mom explained what had happened at the meeting and then became very serious and asked me how I felt about being in a special education math class. She had asked me this before, but this time it was serious. The papers had been signed.

I told her I didn't know, but anything must be better than staying in the class I was in. I felt relieved and excited. We finally had an answer that was official! It was not my fault that I didn't understand math. I have a learning disability. At least now I could explain what was wrong and I didn't have to sit in a classroom where everyone else understood the material and I did not. I knew that I didn't have to feel embarrassed all the time. I didn't care what some people thought. I had just gone from feeling completely out of control in my life to suddenly being able to identify what was wrong! I had something concrete to tell them — my friends, my teachers, my parents — all of them. I am bad at math because my brain just wasn't wired to do it, not because I am dumb or a failure.

Most of all, this meeting validated that my problem was real. There really had been something wrong with me all this time. It wasn't my fault that I didn't understand math, and now everyone knew that. I felt strangely light, airy, as if I could leave the ground any minute. The muscles in my face began to relax, a weight had been lifted. I was exhilarated by the idea that I wouldn't have to take algebra. And while I knew I would turn some heads by showing up in the special education math class, I was up for the challenge.

Rows of white, flat-surfaced desks, posters with kittens and puppies and slogans that read SMILE *or* WHEN YOU'RE FEELING DOWN LOOK UP. *A number line running the length of the chalkboard, along with a row of cursive letters in the order of the alphabet. All of this comes into view as I turn the corner into the special education classroom for the first time.*

I feel drawn toward the front of the room and, finding a desk, I swing my backpack off my shoulder and lean it up against the leg of my chair. Before looking around, I rifle for my pen and notebook and place them on my desk. I know that most of the students in this class will look at me and wonder why I am here. I know that most people view me as smart and conscientious. I am friends with a "good" set of students, well behaved, respectful, most think I get straight A's. I also know that most of the students in this class are considered "bad," the kids that make trouble, fight, beat people up, smoke in the bathroom. These are the kids who don't fit in, that the teachers don't like.

And I also know that this could go a couple of ways: Either I'll assimilate into the group by working hard at not standing out or making others feel uncomfortable or odd, as if they are being judged by me. Or I'll appear as an intruder, an uninvited, untrusted outsider, and no one will let their guard down.

I am the first person here. No teacher, no students. The halls are still pulsing. I begin to scratch the date onto the top of my notebook paper when I hear rustling and catch a dark, hunched figure hurriedly slipping in from the hallway. Head bent, darting like an exposed, helpless animal toward the nearest rock or hiding place, he collapses into a desk along the wall in the far corner of the room. His head remains down, his shoulders hunched as he awkwardly plunges into his bag and shuffles through papers with nervous speed. His eyes are like a rabbit's, stealing quick furtive glances from under the bill of his hat. His clothes are shabby and outdated. His coat, an old, quilted, snowmobile jacket, too warm for early fall, hangs loosely over his bent form like a beetle shell. He has thick glasses with dark rims, a shaggy growth of curly beard hair, and unwashed, unkempt curls spill out from under the back of his baseball cap.

There is a yell out in the hallway. As I turn toward the entryway, Justin — dark, swarthy, and loud — comes rushing in. A troublemaker from my science class, he pauses only to throw his folder from the back of the room to his desk toward the front and with a whoop he jumps onto his chair and squats there for a second before his legs fall out from under him and he ends up with his butt in the seat. Justin instantly notices the black shadow in the corner who lifts his head just long enough to watch Justin's acrobatics with wonder and admiration. "Hey there, Randy."

Justin nods toward the hunched figure who gives a quick smile back in acknowledgment.

I feel as if something isn't right, something is off, and then I realize that the words I just heard, said in a kind, sincere way, had just come out of the same person who did nothing but poke fun and taunt people in his other classes. If anything, Randy appeared like the perfect prey for someone like Justin. I wait for a follow-up insult but it never comes. Justin's eyes turn toward me with a surprised and curious look, but he doesn't say anything and my eyes return to my paper, where I begin to run my pen across the page making distracted thoughtless designs.

I hear Tanya before I see her. Loud, with overdone, dyed red hair, bird-nest bangs, caked-on eye makeup, cheap, too-tight jeans, and a tight red T-shirt under a denim jacket. She is one of the baddest of the bad girls in school. She enters the room in close conversation with a tall thin girl with stringy blond hair, dark circles under her eyes, and an empty mean look, a wildcat edge, with a slight bulge in her abdomen. So this is the thirteen-year-old I have heard whispered about by teachers and students. People shaking their heads in disapproval. The thirteen-year-old who is pregnant. I watch Justin watching them with an abandoned look of wonder, and a bit of bashfulness falls over his expression as he acknowledges their entry.

Justin greets someone named Mindy. I look up and see a girl who looks familiar. I have seen her before, or glimpses of her, alone in the hallway between classes, or in the cafeteria, eating in silence. Overweight, with big, outdated glasses that cover her face, she has a poufy perm and wears a hot-pink sweatshirt with puffy, painted kittens and turquoise sweatpants.

She is another person ripe for Justin's taunting. "Hey there, Mindy."

Justin casts her a look and a big, winning smile that shows all of his teeth. She smiles back bashfully and gratefully at him. Her eyes catch a glimpse of me and instantly fall; her countenance closes up with something like self-consciousness and confusion. I do that to her, I represent an entire group of people who make someone like Mindy feel embarrassed and ashamed. For the first time during this experience, I realize just how much of an outsider I am and how I am perceived without even speaking.

Yet even as an outsider in this group, I already feel more at ease here than in any of my other classes. Through the very act of being here I am admitting that I don't understand math. Maybe I do not have to fake anything here. Maybe for the first time in ages I can just be me.

Young, with blond curly hair, Mrs. Massaroni hurriedly enters the room. She is greeted by most of the students who have had her before, and she smiles back while making her way to the front of the room carrying a stack of photocopied sheets. She apologizes for being late, explaining that there was a line at the copier. She begins to pass out the work sheets. She is young, but there is a toughness about her that demands respect and one gets the feeling that her praise has to be earned, but she isn't cold, hard, or mean. She does, however, have expectations from which she won't budge. She explains that these sheets will be something we do every day. She calls them review sheets. We are not competing with one another but with ourselves.

I look around and I feel heartened by the realization that no one else in this room gets it either. That we all struggle with math and it's OK. The realization is comforting, freeing. For the first time in my life the pressure is off. I can breathe. I am not expected to get it, in fact it's OK that I don't, and I am not in the minority. No one around me is whispering about *how easy this is or how they "know the answer." The questions I want to ask aren't dumb and it's all right if I ask them over and over again. Mrs. Massaroni doesn't expect me to understand it the first time, and I am not the only one. I feel relaxed, at ease, older somehow and for the first time in a long time, in control of myself.*

Here, after all those years of fear and withdrawal, I can finally start raising my hand in class again.

Returning home after my first day in special education math class, I felt a calm I had forgotten was possible. I felt confident, a safe, solid feeling. For the first time in a very, very long time — so long, in fact, that it felt as if the memory may have really been a dream — I felt like a wide-open plain inside, relaxed, empowered. I didn't feel afraid anymore. I had no idea life could feel so good.

Something else amazing and unexpected happened. Within three days of attending my special education math class, my panic attacks stopped. Just like that. I no longer went to bed scared or dreaded the idea of going to school. Months of counseling without ever reaching an answer, and here was the explanation — my anxiety was connected to my learning disability. All this time, my fear of my unnamed demons had been the main instigator of my panic attacks. I still felt anxious, especially in social situations and felt I had to be constantly vigilant to keep it under control, but my night attacks weren't happening anymore. I could hardly believe it.

When my friends asked what math class I was in, I told them

right away, "Special education math." I honestly enjoyed being able to tell them the truth. I never once worried about what they would think. I was proud of being in special education because it was where I needed to be. And they knew me. They knew I was bright and intelligent and could be fun. Those things didn't change just because I attended a different math class. Besides, I was reveling in relief and my new feelings of empowerment.

My parents were relieved and happy with the change. Mom continued reading and researching to learn more about my disability and LD in general. I was still hesitant to try new things, to go out to public places alone, and I avoided social situations like dances and parties, but now it wasn't so much because I was afraid of getting sick, but more because I was afraid of how far behind I had fallen, how much further along everyone else was. I wouldn't know what to do with myself at a party or social event. It was more a fear of not knowing how to behave, because I had missed out on the practice.

But for me, this caution was minor. I could eat again. I could sleep again. I was not terrified anymore. I don't think it's an exaggeration to say that special education saved my life.

Becoming an Author

DURING EIGHTH GRADE I

continued to write poetry and

Mrs. Williams continued to act

as a mentor, encouraging me, pro-

viding feedback, and editing the

pieces I produced. Our summer

work together had been success-

ful on all levels. My self-esteem

was gradually improving.

We were building a collection of poems, images, and stories. The process was frustrating at times, but being involved with a group of adults in a creative endeavor was very rewarding to me and added greatly to my newly found sense of confidence and control.

By winter, talk of possibly grouping my poems and Charlie's images together to make a book became more and more frequent, and everyone involved was excited at the prospect. The idea of a book thrilled me. Becoming an author would fulfill the mantras I had comforted myself with all these years. It seemed to affirm: "Yes, you are special, you are meant for bigger things."

Mrs. Williams and I had not yet presented what I had written to Charlie, and we weren't sure what he would think of my writing. We were concerned that he wouldn't feel my poems resonated with the ideas he wished to express through his paintings. When we finally showed the collection of art and writing to Charlie, we all waited in suspense for his reaction. We were delighted when he announced that he was amazed by how closely my writing had captured in words the thoughts, moods, themes, and feelings he had intended to convey in his paintings. In fact, Charlie was especially moved by one of my poems; he said it helped him solve a problem he had been struggling with in one of his paintings. He decided to repaint the painting using the ideas he gained from the poem.

As our pile of collaborative writing and art grew, the idea of creating a book ripened and flourished, in spite of initial feedback urging caution. Friends in the publishing industry were discouraging, claiming that poetry and art books rarely sell well and are always difficult and costly to produce and market. Regardless, my mom kept thinking that we had something interesting on our hands and that we should expand its audience beyond friends and family.

Through the Learning Disabilities Association newsletter, my mom learned that Dr. Susan Baum, the person whose research was the catalyst for our new understanding of my learning difference, was scheduled to be a speaker at the next LDA conference in Michigan. Mom realized that my book project was a perfect example of the puzzling paradox of the gifted and learning disabled whom Susan wrote about in her article. The project demonstrated clearly that by focusing on someone's strengths you can help them deal with their weaknesses. The book's purpose became clear. The poetry and art seemed to be a powerful combination but the book's true message was about education, the cracks in the system, and the critical need for alternative approaches. With a much more clear focus, we put together a manuscript that not only featured my writing and Charlie's art, but also wrapped itself around my educational experiences and what we had learned about learning disabilities over years of trying to work within the traditional system.

With the rough manuscript in hand, Mom attended the LDA conference, soliciting reactions from the LD experts, including Susan Baum. All of the educational professionals who read it were very excited and encouraging of the project. Mom felt so strongly about the message the book would convey, she decided that if we couldn't find a publisher, we would just have to publish the book ourselves. She immediately embarked on a quest to teach herself all about book publishing, networking tirelessly with authors, editors, publishers, printers. As her crash course progressed, she grew more and more confident that we could turn this book idea into reality.

By the end of my eighth-grade year, my parents, my grandfather, Charlie, and Mrs. Williams decided to jump off a steep financial cliff and self-publish the book. We researched the printers in town, worked to perfect the manuscript, revising it several times, and prepared Charlie's paintings for four-color reproduction. I wrote a new poem for the beginning of the book entitled "Self-Portrait." My mom and Mrs. Williams both wrote essays for the book that described their experiences in trying to get me the help I needed to succeed in school. Eventually, we came to the point where everyone was satisfied with the message of the book and Charlie felt happy with the reproduction of his images.

It was an exciting, creative process that at times didn't feel real. However, for me the steady adult support was empowering. I felt like an honorary member of their world — a world where I fit in naturally and easily, in contrast to my school world, where I felt like I was always struggling to maintain day-to-day relationships with my peers.

Finally, the book, titled *What Once Was White*, was ready to be printed. One night in the fall of my ninth-grade year, we all went to the printer together to watch the pages as they started to roll off the press. I remember that night well.

The chemical and ink fumes are overwhelming. They permeate everything in the harshly lit printing warehouse and I feel light-headed. I stand next to some empty pigment cans and watch as the giant roaring and turning press sends pages of my book shooting out onto a wooden flat.

My poetry, which has always been printed on cheap computer paper, is now being printed onto a glossy, heavy stock. The letters once formed in thin, dot matrix characters are now printed in a large, round font, widely spaced and assertive on the page. Every word of every poem I know by heart, but as they fall evenly out of the mouth of the machine, they are rendered foreign to me in their new, polished, printed finish.

I assume that when one's book is first published, the author feels excited, an electric rush of intense joy. Outwardly, I smile excitedly and I toast the successful completion of the book with my parents, Mr. and Mrs. Williams, Charlie and his wife, Carrie, raising Dixie cups of grape juice and champagne. Inside, I feel a sinking sense of disillusionment. I had participated in the book's design and had been at the printer for almost every stage of its production. Now, watching the broad sheets roll off the press, it seems like nothing more than ink and paper. Nothing special. There isn't any magic. No sense of having accomplished something out of the ordinary.

Rationally, I realize that I am accomplishing something at fifteen that other people may spend their whole lives striving for. But I feel numb and apathetic. So this is it, I ponder. Surround some nice paper with fancy cardboard and a little glue and you have a book. *I also wonder about what publishing a book and being an author will mean for me in the future. How will it change things for me? Will the book be successful? It doesn't seem real, but I am an author now.*

Before making the final decision to publish the book, my parents drilled me with questions. They wanted to know how I would feel being known as the learning disabled girl at school, or being openly and publicly labeled. They worried about my ability to handle potentially embarrassing headlines, such as "Gimp Does Good," as my dad jokingly suggested. They wondered if I would be able to talk about my disability or my status as an author. How would I answer questions or face the skepticism of others? How would I feel if my friends suddenly felt intimidated by me because I had written a book?

I reassured my parents that I could handle it, that I was strong, and that I didn't mind what people called me. I did my best to convince them — and myself — that I could deal with whatever happened.

I'm not sure any of us thought that the publication of the book would result in the barrage of requests for me to come tell my story to groups of parents, kids, teachers, and special educators. Honestly, I wasn't sure how I would hold up under these pressures, or if I could handle publicly talking about my learning disability. For so many years, I had been unable to describe my learning disability to anyone or share what it was like for me to get through a typical day. I wasn't able to tell my friends or my family. But now I was asked to get up in front of a room full of strangers and talk about all these things and how they affected me. Could I do it?

Over the years, I had been intensely silent in my classes, rarely, if ever, speaking or raising my hand. Even when I knew the correct answer or had something to say, I kept it to myself. I saw the book as an opportunity to show others what was going on inside me, to show everyone that I was more than just the silent girl in class. I wanted to show them that I did have ideas. The book became my chance to have a voice, to speak. While I couldn't predict how I would feel about the book or talking about my learning disability, I had made up my mind that I could handle anything in exchange for this opportunity to be heard. This seemed like what I had been waiting for. I had gone through so much. Here was my chance to let others know what it was like.

It is late spring and the first bound copy of the book has arrived special delivery from the bindery in New Jersey. It is the same day I am scheduled to give a presentation on the book with Mrs. Williams at the local high school. This is going to be my first presentation, and it is going to be my first time speaking publicly about my learning disability.

Mom picks me up from the junior high and we drive to the high school. Walking in, seeing the tables and chairs placed for people, I feel my throat constrict and my pulse quicken. I am nervous, and I can tell my mom is nervous for me. Soon, teachers and staff members file in. It is not a large audience, but according to the school librarian, it's a bigger turnout than usual. I hang back, leaning against a table in the front of the room, while Mrs. Williams speaks. She talks about working with me on the book, about her role in its creation, and about how teachers can best help students like me. I don't hear much of what is said — I am too nervous, too concerned with how I must look to everyone sitting out there. I am too afraid, too focused on what I am going to say. I am prepared to talk a little about my LD, a little about the process of making a book, and a little about my writing. Mrs. Williams finishes and then introduces me. She sits down, and I stand there alone.

Stepping forward, I lift my head and survey the room. I sense there is a general question hanging in the minds of the teachers who sit before me. They are all asking, "Can she do it?" At that moment all of my nervous anxiety leaves. I step forward and feel myself assuming a familiar role, like I did as a child when I played "pretend." Yet this role does not feel like pretend, it feels normal, natural, like a strong heroine taking her stand. I feel beautiful, powerful, wise, kind — as if I have found myself. I feel unbelievably alert and calm.

I begin by talking about my learning disability. I try to think of examples that others can relate to. I talk about it being like Alzheimer's: One minute you know something and the next you don't. I talk about how hard basic tasks are for me, such as telling time, dialing a phone, and spelling simple words. I talk about dreading being called on in math class.

As I speak, my communication skills grow. The act of taking my thoughts and putting them into words helps relieve my anxiety. With each sentence, I feel the energy from the audience increase. I draw on that energy and notice them become more and more rapt in attention. I read their reactions while I speak. If I get an approving nod or positive reaction to something being said, I elaborate. When I see I am losing them with vague description, I let it drop and move on to something else.

When I finish talking about the book project and my learning disability, I invite questions. I find that I am loving this challenge of thinking on my feet and responding. Soon someone asks if I would read one of the poems from the book, and I decide to read the poem "Wellspring."

I had read this poem several times aloud to myself as I was writing it. I always write my poems in a certain voice, to a certain rhythm, and while I write, I read them out loud to myself. I know the poem is good when it flows just right and the words fit my sense of rhythm for the piece. However, I had never read any of my poems out loud to anyone else before — certainly never to a room full of adults.

I open the book to the right page and, as I begin to read, the audience disappears. It is just me and the page, the poem, the words, the feelings that go with them. I read slowly, pronouncing each word, knowing where I want each line, each inflection, and each pause. For the first time, I read out loud publicly in a voice matching my internal one.

WELLSPRING

If you want to fill the well, make a boat out of paper,
set it on a dry and dusty riverbed,
cracked and wrinkled like the face of a grandmother.
Lie down on its fragile planks,

spread your hair over the edge like ivy
to cling to the broken sand.

Let your thoughts begin to trickle
as if they were rain,
soaking your clothes and hair
until you feel yourself begin to drift along
on the current of ideas
like a leaf fallen on a river.

Spinning across reflections of the sky
and eddying through the willows,
find the current below you,
seeking its way into the ancient stone edifice of the well,
pouring into its empty circle
just as love pours into an empty heart.

The well becomes full
and your words are lifted in a bucket —
brought into the sunlight
where the thirsty dip their hands in and drink.

It's silent after I finish. Then sound returns. I look at my parents' faces
and see expressions of shock. The audience claps. A few have tears in their
eyes. I am asked to read more, and I do.

* * *

The response from my presentation was overwhelming. People complimented me on the reading of my poems and talked about how valuable it was for them to hear about having a learning disability from a student's perspective. My mom and dad both said later that when I spoke, it was as if I became a completely different person. I realized that I was good at this. I was good at thinking on my feet and communicating. I liked the feeling of power and energy I got from the audience in the room. I liked seeing the expression on their faces when I got up and read a poem I had written.

Soon we were flooded with invitations for me to speak at local elementary schools and teachers' meetings. Every speech I did was an improvement over the last. I would change and modify the content and extend it with new insights about my own LD.

But even though I felt confident and excited while speaking, it was also a draining experience. Every time I told my story, I would, in a way, relive it all over again, taking myself along with the audience on a roller coaster of emotions. There was a cost to this authenticity. I always complained of headaches afterward and felt exhausted. I also remember feeling intensely lonely. I would give a presentation to a group of 300 teachers or to three classes of sixth graders, and then realize that I would probably never see any of these people again. I felt like I was bleeding out my personal story, giving so much of myself, and not getting enough back in return. At the end, after all the applause and adulation, everyone just walked away, leaving me alone.

All summer, along with speaking, I also did book signings at local bookstores and many interviews with local media. I traveled to art fairs and sold my book from a makeshift booth next to my mom's batik booth. Response to the book was overwhelming. I was bombarded by people who had stories of their own experiences and struggles with learning difficulties or of family members, children, or friends who struggled. Teachers and school administrators also bought books, expressing their desire to learn more about LD and what they could do to help. Many people thanked me for championing the cause and were impressed by what I had accomplished. I finally woke up to what people were giving back to me: their own stories! After almost every interview or speech or book signing, people would send me letters of appreciation. They were sending moving tributes and sharing their own touching stories, even when they had not yet met me.

> Dear Samantha, I read your story and when I read "whether you're seven or seventy (I am 68), one day you'll find a place where you excel," I sobbed. Thank you so much for passing on those encouraging words.

> I am twelve years old and in the seventh grade. I am LD in math. My teacher helped me understand that it was not

my fault. When I read your book I was so touched because I knew now that I am not the only one who felt that they are dumb and lazy. In my regular class I didn't put my hand up very much. Here I put my hand up the whole time. I didn't tell any of my friends about my LD because I thought they would laugh. I know you won't laugh. Well, bye now.

I just finished reading your book for the third time. You signed it for me "Never Give Up." Samantha, you didn't know it, but I've seriously been thinking about giving up a whole lot of things — my teaching is one of them. I'm tired, and teaching can be draining. But after reading your work, and remembering how much I prize all kinds of learning, especially when it comes in special combinations, I have decided to hang in there. Your strength has given me courage to try some more.

I was so touched by the article. I have a learning disabled daughter and had to battle an indifferent school system while her self-esteem ebbed away. She is still suffering the aftereffects of teachers whose attitude was "If she would just try a little harder." At times she felt no one believed in her but me. Fortunately, she has a talent to help heal the wounds of what she can't do. She is an athlete and she can run like the wind. Congratulations on winning your war.

Too many parents are so immobilized that they can only wring their hands and cannot speak up for their kids.

Dear Sam. My student teacher gave me your book. She said it represented what I had taught her. I was touched. I am a mother of two daughters and a seventeen-year veteran teacher. Your words and images made my feelings about the sacredness of life and the importance of honoring all children come alive again. I know we all carry beautiful gifts within us, and if we're fortunate someone helps us discover them.

My father is eighty-five. I know my time with this gentle man is limited. When I read "The Cloak," I knew I had found the poem to read at his service when the time comes. Your poem "Self-Portrait" reminds me of all the ways we try to say our names so others will listen and know who we are. Thanks for the beauty of your words and the sensitivity of your soul. I wish every teacher could read this and understand the difference they can make in the lives of children.

Thank you for the privilege of hearing your story. I was baby-sitting and noticed your book on the coffee table. As I read, my eyes welled with tears. You have touched my heart and changed me forever. I plan to pursue a career in special education. You have shown me that the greatest thing I could ever do for my students is believe in them. I promise you that I will try to find the good in each and every child who crosses my path during my life.

I was energized by the wonderful effect my book and my story was having on people. It was more than I had hoped for. I felt connected to so many who had experiences and feelings similar to mine. Now, perfect strangers of all ages were opening up and trusting me with their most private life stories and struggles and, by sharing my story, the lives of others were being changed.

Making a Difference

BY THE END OF THE

summer before tenth grade,

three months after we had

begun to sell *What Once Was*

White, we sold out of all 3,000

copies. At that point, we decided

that the book publishing and

marketing business was not

for us.

Our living room had become a book warehouse, with every inch of floor space filled with boxes of books, orders and invoices, packing cartons, and tape. The phone was always ringing with various book-related requests. Fortunately for us, not long after this decision, we received a call from Don Tubesing, publisher at Pfeifer-Hamilton, a small company in Minnesota known nationally for their award-winning picture books featuring beautiful artwork and important messages. They learned about the book when my mom sent a copy to their editor, in appreciation for her earlier assistance with Mom's crash course in publishing.

Don told us that the staff at Pfeifer-Hamilton was very impressed with our book, believed in its message, and wanted to help it reach a broader audience. We were thrilled with their interest, and my mom, Mrs. Williams, and I traveled to Duluth and met with Don, his wife, Nancy, and the rest of the Pfeifer-Hamilton team.

Don and Nancy's belief in the project and its message was sincere and moving. While I was there, sitting across the meeting room table or at dinner, I watched these two creative, innovative, caring people and was blown away by their excitement and their capacity to be turned on by ideas. I remember feeling inspired and wishing I could be like them when I grew up. I was flattered and ecstatic that they cared and that everyone loved the book and my writing. All of it seemed to be happening in some kind of dream. Pfeifer-Hamilton agreed to carry out the second printing of the book. They gave the book a facelift, redesigned its shape slightly and changed the title to *Reach for the Moon*.

Once the new book was printed, the publisher sent me on a five-city media tour. The summer between tenth and eleventh grade, my mom joined me on a whirlwind book tour to Philadelphia, Baltimore, Washington, D.C., St. Louis, and Minneapolis. It was an intense two weeks out on the road: endless TV, radio, and newspaper interviews, a swirl of escorts, hotels, food, telling and retelling my story over and over again. Exhausting — but also exhilarating. Everywhere we went, people connected to my story and were touched by what I had to say.

I was flattered by the positive press for *Reach for the Moon* and stunned by the awards the book received, but the whole experience of being an author and a public speaker still felt unreal to me and disconnected from my life at home and school. For much of the time, the meaning of the book and the reasons why we produced it felt lost, too. But every time I really connected with an audience or with an individual at a book signing, it all became worthwhile again.

People kept lining up, not just to purchase the book and not just to ask me a question, but to tell me their story, or to tell me the story of their son or daughter, or niece or nephew, or grandchild. Everyone, it seemed, knows and loves somebody who has struggled with learning in the traditional manner, and thus struggled with failure and low self-confidence. My story and *Reach for the Moon* seemed to give them a sense of hope and offered them a treasure they could pass on to their loved ones who learned differently.

I had one woman tell me that her daughter struggled so much with forming letters that her teacher told her she could never be a writer. But after reading my book, she was determined not to let her disability stop her. Now she has a teacher whom she dictates her stories to, and recently she had one published in a school newsletter.

Ever since the book was released, I had been approached by people whose lives were in some way affected by learning differences. Most were desperate parents who wanted to tell me about their child's difficulties, grasping at anything they could to help their child drowning in a school system that didn't understand. Families struggling with teachers, teachers at their wits' end struggling with families. Many would begin to cry as they spoke and I learned early on that what many of these people needed most was someone who understood the pain and who would listen to them — someone they could express their anger and helplessness to. I still did not fully comprehend just how powerful my book could be for others. What was it that I had done to cause people to feel so connected to me, what was it that was so significant?

In the last city on our tour, and at one of our last book signings, I met someone who made it very clear to me.

I sit at a long, low table looking out through large windows that face the street. The sun is setting and the sky shows wisps of gold and orange that fade into searing pink. I watch my mom wander through the store.

Charlie, who is also signing books with me, gets up from the table to stretch and look around.

When we first arrived at the bookstore, a few people were waiting to have their books signed. An elderly woman with stark white hair and pink, wrinkled skin asked us to sign a book for her autistic grandson who lived in Texas. I signed another for a little boy and his sister who only timidly approached the table at their mother's urging. There were a few more, a couple of schoolteachers, the bookstore owner's wife, one for a woman who just loved the art. Now, the bookstore is empty except for the three of us whiling away the time until we can leave.

This is the last stop on the tour. My smile feels mechanical to me now, and it seems as if there is a barrier between me and the world. I feel remote, dazed, everything is one big blur.

As I sit here looking out the windows watching the sky grow darker, a middle-aged man approaches the table and picks up a book. He is wearing a Bruegger's Bagel T-shirt and khaki shorts. He has glasses and dark, thinning hair combed over to one side. I smile at him and offer to answer any questions he might have. He asks if he can take a book somewhere quiet to read it. I nod and he wanders behind some shelves. I get up, walk around a bit, flip through some children's books. I sign another two books — one for a little girl who hopes to be a writer someday and another for a teacher who wants to use the book in his classroom to teach his kids about creative writing. Then the local newspaper reporter comes in and asks me questions and takes my picture with Charlie and my mom.

I return to my autographing post and start doodling on a piece of paper when the bagel T-shirt man, whom I assumed had left the store, walks over and kneels down in front of the table looking up into my face. My first re-action is to smile and I begin to, but stop this now-automatic reaction when I see his face.

There is something unusual about this man's expression. I realize that he has been crying and is even now fighting back tears. He blurts out halt-ingly, "I just want you to know that in this moment you have completely changed my life."

His voice chokes, wavers, and he removes his glasses to wipe his eyes. "I am a doctor at a hospital here in town, and I have lived here for years. Every day I have to pull out a road map to figure out how I am going to get to work. All my life there have been these holes — these things I just can't understand or do. I always blamed myself, thought I was a failure. But now, after reading your book, I realize that it isn't my fault — it's because I have a learning disability!"

I take hold of his hand and feel a flood of emotion, tears welling up in my own eyes. I realize that by telling my story, I have given him the same gift I had been given when I discovered that things I couldn't do were not my fault, that I was not a bad person. Sharing my story had lifted that weight, had allowed him to stop beating himself up. I could sense how much that awareness meant to him — because of how much it had meant to me.

For forty-some-odd years, he had seen himself, despite his successes, as less than the rest of the world, defective somehow. He had felt strange, frus-trated, angry with himself, just as I had felt all those years in school. He looked tremendously relieved, and I knew exactly what it was he was *feeling! Looking into this man's eyes, I felt my heart open to his pain — and his new relief, even joy. I understood in that moment why* Reach for the Moon *was so important.*

He bought two books: one for a girl he knew struggling through school and one for himself. I signed them both and he walked over to the counter to pay. Then, meeting my eyes with a significant smile, he thanked me again, turned, and pushed his way out through the door and disappeared from view.

Maybe it was the timing — things had calmed down a bit on the last leg of the tour. Maybe it was his sincerity of feeling, or the fact that this sounded like someone who didn't usually let himself be carried away by emotion. Perhaps it was the clear, simple words he used, "You have completely changed my life." It hit me then. He and everyone like him were my reasons for putting my story out there. The true impact of the book and the importance of its message became clear, and I knew then that it had all been worthwhile. I could die today knowing that I had made a difference.

Still, I could not help but wonder how many thousands, millions of people like him, like me, were out there walking around wounded, lonely, scared, trapped by not understanding what was wrong, feeling as if the dark shadow that plagues them is their fault. I couldn't help but want to find a way to reach out and offer hope to these people who, like me, suffered silently and alone.

Falling Through the Cracks

BUOYED UP BY THE SUCCESS

of the summer book tour, my

transition into high school was

smoother than my shift from

elementary school to junior high.

Over the past three years, I had

grown accustomed to the flow of

a school day, with class changes

and different teachers.

I went into high school with a small but established group of friends and lots of familiar faces. I also entered tenth grade with a new self-assurance gained from my summer spent speaking, giving interviews, and interacting with total strangers at book signings and other events. Not only had I gained a certain level of confidence from my work with the book, I had also deepened my awareness of learning disabilities and the challenges faced by people who have them.

I had to make an intentional shift from being treated as an expert in the field by people who had heard me speak or read my book, back to being a fifteen-year-old high-school student. I strove to normalize my experiences with the book. I made a decision not to talk about it unless asked. In fact, I usually downplayed the book. But my real concern centered more on my ability to fit in and live up to the social expectations of being a tenth grader when I continued to feel nothing but out of place and behind most of my peers.

Walking into my high-school special education class, I was surprised by how different the mood and the students were from what I had experienced in my junior high special education class. There had been a sense of hope in my junior high class, a belief that we simply learned differently but still had opportunities ahead of us. Our teacher had been helpful, encouraging, and relentless in her high expectations and repetitive individualized lesson plans that felt challenging but possible. In junior high special education, even the kids who seemed to have the most hopeless home lives and recurrent behavior issues, still seemed to have a fighting chance and a sense of hope.

However, here, in my high school special education math class, hopelessness smoldered under the fluorescent lighting. The class size was noticeably smaller and my peers filling the seats were silent and withdrawn, sweatshirt hoods and baseball caps shielding their faces. No one interacted. Most were hunched over, heads down on the desk so they could sleep, or wore headphones tuning out the world around them. Justin was the only other student present from our old class. The rest had opted to attend vocational education classes or seemed to have just disappeared. This class felt like a holding tank for people just biding their time until graduation. The system seemed to have given up on these students — and they, in turn, had given up on themselves.

Here was a living example of all the school system special education horror stories I had heard over the past few months as I traveled across the country. Here, filling these chairs were the kids who didn't make it, who were never going to make it. I felt my luck keenly and realized that I was one of the few. I had parents who cared, who were involved, who fought for me, told me it wasn't my fault, and helped me find what it was I could do. They supported me and took an interest in seeing my unique view of the world through my learning disability. I also had teachers who believed in me as well, and who took time to help me be successful. I had been able to skate through as one of the good kids, fitting in where I needed to, even if it was only on the surface.

But these kids hadn't had any of that support or that experience of success. They hadn't comforted themselves with fairy tales of their own greatness to carry them through like I had. There wasn't anyone to give them those illusions. They hadn't felt successful in something and hadn't had their achievements recognized and valued. They had been ridiculed from an early age for their hand-me-down clothes, the trailer they lived in, the mother or father they were missing, or for the fact that they talked differently or they looked different, or didn't learn to read as quickly or answer questions in class. They were class clowns, behavior problems, because that way *they* were in charge of the laughter, they were in control of the inevitable criticism.

Teachers and administrators had given up on them, because these kids couldn't demonstrate what they had never been given — compassion, understanding, respect, love. Consequently, there was nothing to endear them to anybody, nothing to make people want to go out of their way to help them succeed. Special education for these kids was a mark of inability and it virtually guaranteed their defeat. It meant they were defective people who needed to be fixed instead of beautiful individuals who saw the world in a different way.

I had been given so many gifts — and these students so few. Most of these special education classmates were on parole or on court release so they could attend school. I realized as I looked at them, with their hardened "bring it on" attitudes, that for most it was too late. They had been abandoned long ago and, without any other voices to tell them differently, they had given up on themselves. Who could blame them? In junior high, I felt like special education had saved my life. Here in high school, I felt heartsick walking through the doors of this classroom, weighed down with the certainty that my special education classmates did not and probably never would share the hope and the confidence that was beginning to sustain me.

The teacher who had been assigned to our class gave off little energy and lacked any expectations or idea of what to do with us. Her attitude was kind but disinterested. She appeared to be just passing the time, collecting a paycheck. Most class periods were spent in class discussions of various students' legal issues, such as court dates or appeals. Other discussions focused on shared experiences working at local fast-food restaurants or convenience stores. Occasionally, we would go over a math concept or two, but the lesson was usually bogged down or interrupted by students coming in late or leaving early or drifting off into tangents.

In my other classes, I continued to encounter my same difficulties with learning — and with speaking up for myself. While I had become comfortable over the summer speaking openly in public to audiences of hundreds of people regarding my learning disability, describing what it was, how it affected me, as well as the pain I went through and the humiliation I sometimes felt, I still had great difficulty talking about these same issues one-on-one.

I dreaded asking people for the extra help that I needed. I

found the entire process of being a self-advocate awkward, and inexplicably hard, especially when I needed something, such as more time on a test or taking something home to type it on my computer so I could use the spell checker. I was extremely fearful of people thinking that I was trying to get away with something, that I couldn't do it just as well as everyone else in the same amount of time, under the same circumstances. I was still afraid of not living up to my identity as a "smart kid."

Even though I was an advocate and spokesperson for the learning disabled in public, in private I was still ashamed of my inability to keep up with others — and afraid of looking different. I remember one teacher's shocking response when I tried to talk with her about my learning disability.

I am one of the stragglers today, taking more time and care than is needed to put my books back into my backpack, trying to buy myself a little more time while indecision and fear pound and whirl through me. I know I have to do it. I would seem stupid, foolish, scared if I didn't tell her, and even more foolish and scared if it came from my special education teacher or my mom. Besides, if I don't warn her about my LD, it will reveal itself soon enough through assigned graphs or charts, or grammatical errors in lab reports. It's not as if I can pretend that I just forgot about my LD or didn't know I had it.

I look through the open doorway of the science classroom and into the crowded hall. Hundreds of bodies move past, and I am tempted not to go through with this, to just slip out of class. But I can't stand the wait any longer. I cannot face one more day of my mom's nagging, asking me if I have told all of my teachers yet. I swallow hard and sling my backpack over my left shoulder. I approach her desk, trying to look as nonchalant as I can, while each step forward twists my stomach into tighter knots.

Deep down, I think I know what her reaction will be. They all have about the same response. They listen to my explanation, smile, nod, offer to help any way they can, and ask me to be sure to let them know if I have trouble with something in their class. I walk away feeling totally relieved that my confession is over and convinced that I probably won't need any of the help they offer. Even if I did I probably wouldn't ask for it. Self-advocating for me is simply a formality. I will keep up with everyone else, even if it means staying up all night to finish an assignment.

Yet despite the fact I know all this, despite the fact I have never had a negative reaction to my admission of a learning difficulty from any of my teachers, and despite the warm smiles and flaky absentmindedness of the teacher I am about to share this with, I am still as petrified as I was the first time I braved telling someone about my LD. I feel as if I am being forward, as if I am presumptuous in assuming that anyone really cares anything about me. I feel as though I am making excuses for myself.

I reach the front desk just as Mrs. Cook bends her head to look at the attendance sheet to cross a name out. I say her name, my tongue dry in my mouth. I say it too gently, she doesn't look up. I say it again a little louder. She raises her head this time and her kind, inquisitive eyes look up at me, a smile spreading across her face in acknowledgment.

I try to keep my eyes focused on hers since this is what people who have nothing to hide do, but despite my efforts, my eyes look down at the desk as

I begin to describe my learning disability to her. I quickly add at the end that it shouldn't be too much of a problem unless I have to work with graphs or do equations for experiments. I am angry at how fast my words have left my mouth, feeling like the speed may have revealed that I am nervous.

I stop talking and slowly bring my eyes up again to meet hers. In a kind voice, Mrs. Cook thanks me for telling her. She says she wants to help me however she can and that if I need to stay after class and ask questions she will be happy to stay after as well.

Her reaction is the one I expected. In fact, I barely hear what she says as my pounding heartbeat slows and the weight of my sense of responsibility lifts. I feel at once infinitely lighter. I have done my part, said what I am supposed to say, and now no one can hold me at fault for not speaking up.

I come back to myself and feel more and more in control, ready to answer any questions she may have before I leave for my next class. I see a question forming as she continues to look at me. Her eyebrows lift together, a confused, puzzled expression passes over her face and she blurts out, "You have a learning disability? But you can't be learning disabled ... I mean ... you don't look it at all!"

Outwardly, I remain poised and calm, but inwardly I am struck, as the full meaning of her comment unfolds in my mind. I have answered questions like this in TV interviews with news anchors who knew nothing about learning disabilities and were just puppets to their computerized cue cards. I have heard similar remarks or seen surprise in people's eyes when they learned that Sam Abeel, an A student in English and history, and winner of several writing awards, is in a special education math class and has trouble with something as simple as telling time. But I have never heard ignorance about learning disabilities expressed so directly, so innocently. There is a child's wondering look on Mrs. Cook's face, a guileless expression that reveals no ill will or contempt, just surprise and curiosity. As if it were as simple as saying that I had my third and fourth eye removed and that's why I look so normal — but I can't do math.

I answer her question patiently and calmly, wanting to cause her as little embarrassment as possible but also wanting to get my point across. I explain that many people with learning disabilities are average to above average students. They can achieve good grades in many of their academic areas and may not show any outward signs that they learn differently. She doesn't contradict me, but I know I haven't even begun to scratch the surface of the well-worn stereotypes she associates with anyone who learns differently or who is a student in special education.

Deeply disturbed by the powerful hold stereotypes have, I thank Mrs. Cook again, walk out of the room and into the hallway, joining the throng of students pushing toward their next class.

I had fielded comments similar to my science teacher's from people during speaking engagements or book signings. Just as innocently and earnestly they would raise their hands or approach the table and ask questions like: "So when did you get cured of your LD?" or "You're only LD from eight to three during school hours, aren't you? I mean, it doesn't affect your private life, does it?" Both of these questions reveal the askers' ignorance and preconceived ideas of what it means to be learning disabled. But nothing stuck with me or expressed the stereotypes more clearly than my science teacher's question.

Mrs. Cook's comment followed me to my regular education English class that day. Looking around at all the faces, I began to wonder how many of these supposedly "average" students were in fact learning disabled. How many were struggling through their day secretly thinking they were dumb? How many needed help they would never get because, like me, they didn't "look like they could be in special education"? It was these misperceptions that allowed so many people to fall through the cracks and why so many adults had fought to keep me out of special education.

Ongoing Struggles

ACADEMICS WEREN'T THE

only thing I struggled with.

Ever since I could remember,

I have felt uncomfortable in

public places — especially when

I'm alone. I have always felt

self-conscious, and typically only

liked to go out if someone was

with me.

I hated going to the store to buy music, a book, clothes, groceries. Not unlike my aversion to self-advocating and asking for help in school, I also disliked the idea of people finding out that I didn't get things that were so simple for everyone else — like comparing prices, or figuring out a fifteen percent tip, or knowing if twenty dollars is enough to buy two CDs. I was afraid of what others might think of a high-school student who couldn't even count change.

I knew that to a store clerk I looked normal. Yet, when she would ask me for forty-eight cents and I couldn't count out the change in my hand, I would panic and feel humiliated, ashamed, guilty. And if I tried to explain, I was convinced she wouldn't believe me or understand my problem. I avoided purchasing things whenever possible and when I did, I only used big bills — too ashamed of my inability to count change. To this day, my stomach clutches in dread every time I approach a cash register.

Standing in the checkout line, all my movements seem exaggerated, awkward. I feel as if I am onstage, like I don't belong, as if everyone is staring at me and judging me. I think they all see the stain on my shirt or that my jacket doesn't match. A thousand eyes seem to scrutinize my appearance, confirming my every insecurity. My lips get dry, I don't know where to look, because someone will read my glance, interpret it, judge me, know that I don't know what I am doing. I wait for the woman ahead of me to finish writing out her check. I wait for my test.

The woman moves out of view, bags rumpling. With stifled breath, I step up to the counter and place the items down. It feels reassuring to have something to do, but then I begin to feel self-conscious that I am taking too long at the counter. The store clerk finishes ringing up the total.

I open my wallet as he announces it: "Fifteen twenty-eight" — fifteen dollars and twenty-eight cents. I have a twenty. I go blank. I don't know if it's enough. To stall, I repeat back the total to make sure I have it right. The woman behind me suddenly feels very close, as if she were pressing against me. I can hear and feel the impatience in her breathing and the rumpling of her shopping bags. A few seconds stretch into forever. I feel like everyone behind me is becoming hostile and impatient with me. Shame flushes into my cheeks.

I look down, hesitate for a second, and pull out the twenty. For an instant, my heart stops. All sound retreats. Everything feels as if it is moving in slow motion as I hand the clerk the twenty-dollar bill and watch his reaction, waiting to read the unspoken signs that I haven't given him enough. He glances at it, accepts it, and turns to the register.

Instantly, the world resumes its movement in real time, and the knot in my stomach unravels. All the pushing impatience of the bodies behind me fades away. They feel like ordinary people waiting their turn. I can breathe again. I smile, say "Thank you," and walk out. Once again I have just barely escaped disaster.

It wasn't just the obvious things — my inability to correct my own papers for spelling and grammar or my difficulty at completing a graph in science class — that made me feel anxious or worried and ate away at my confidence and self-esteem during high school. It was the small things that unnerved me, the seemingly simple concepts that I couldn't forgive myself for not comprehending.

One of the persistent challenges resulting from my learning disability involved time. Because I don't have any real sense of time, I had trouble planning and structuring my day. I was dependent on help from my mom, which was extremely frustrating as a teenager. I remember one day in particular when I was scheduled to baby-sit at 3:00 in the afternoon.

Typically, if I had something scheduled anytime during the day, I would be careful not to make plans to do anything else, because I could never judge if I would have enough time. When my mom asked me if I wanted to run some errands and then go out to lunch with her that morning, I told her I couldn't because I needed to take a shower before I had to baby-sit at 3:00. She tried to explain that 3:00 was five hours away and that I would have plenty of time to take care of all that stuff before having to leave. I believed her and understood that she was undoubtedly right, but it was humiliating that I couldn't figure it out for myself. Here I was, a junior in high school, and I couldn't even plan my day!

How was I ever going to make it on my own or be independent if I couldn't carry out the basic skills of living? I looked around and everyone else seemed to get it, to be moving forward. I was seventeen and I still wasn't confident driving a car by myself. I hated driving, it made me feel nervous and inadequate. It seemed like all the other drivers on the road were angry with me, that they could tell I didn't know what I. was doing. Driving alone was terrifying and I was completely afraid of screwing up. I couldn't keep all the rules straight in my head. What did a blinking red light mean versus a solid red versus a blinking yellow? I always got mixed up between my left and right and couldn't remember whose turn it was to go at various intersections, who had the right-of-way and when.

I tried to learn to drive a stick shift first, but I couldn't process all of the movements in the order they needed to happen. Shift, let up on the clutch, pay attention to other traffic, the light, knowing when to shift gears. So instead, I was relegated to driving the automatic, but I still struggled with the rest.

I felt foolish about my difficulties driving, as well as envious and intimidated by my friends who confidently got into the front seat of their family cars and ran errands or helped by picking up siblings at school. They begged to drive, craved it, and were already campaigning for first cars of their own so they could drive themselves to school. I, on the other hand, avoided getting behind the wheel and feigned disinterest, when really I was paralyzed by fear. My parents tried to be patient at first, and they understood why a stick shift was difficult for me, but after a while they began to push, wanting me to drive to the convenience store for milk or to pick up Zac from basketball practice, regardless of my excuses and protestations.

In general, my family worried about me and wanted to help, but instead of helping, often their concern only made things harder. They loved me and they wanted for me what everyone else my age seemed to have — friends, a boyfriend, parties to go to, events to be a part of. My parents wanted me to be happy, but what they didn't realize was that as they pushed me to change, it felt like they were not accepting me as I was. When they failed to acknowledge my anxiety about participating in normal every-day activities, no matter how ridiculous my worries may have sounded, I ended up feeling guilty and inadequate for not wanting those very normal things for myself, too.

I felt like a strange outsider everywhere, and I began to beat myself up internally, chastising myself for not being more like my friends, and for being afraid all the time. Those who loved me did what came naturally — they pushed, thinking that if they just pushed hard enough, and reasoned enough, and disregarded all of my excuses and explanations as silly and made up, they would eventually talk me out of my hermit-like existence and convince me I was wrong.

But instead, I began to feel even more insecure and unsure. Already I knew I wasn't normal, and here was more evidence. I continued to scold myself for not being like everyone else. I avoided telling my parents about invitations I received to friends' houses, and didn't tell them about the dances at school, even though they inevitably found out later from friends.

When my parents did get wind of an invitation, they reminded me that the only way I would have friends was if I put the effort into making them. They told me I wouldn't get invited to do things if I always said no.

It was especially hard when my younger brother, Zac, began to do all the things I was afraid of. Everything I found difficult seemed to come so easily to him. He thought nothing of going to the store by himself or running errands. And when he got his driver's training license he was eager and happy to get on the road and start driving himself around.

Zac didn't just have a few close friends, he had several — along with tons of acquaintances. These friends and acquaintances were constantly coming and going in a steady stream, and the phone never stopped ringing for him. From the outside, his relationships looked effortless and stress-free, while mine felt like a lot of work. My little brother was popular, always going to dances and parties and trying out for sports teams.

It was all I could do to leave the house to take the dog for a walk alone. All through my sophomore and junior years I still went clothes shopping with my mom, went to movies with my parents and their friends. I felt comfortable with adults. I could relate to them and felt safe knowing that I wouldn't be pressured into situations where I might feel uncomfortable.

It was especially hard for my dad to understand my hesitancy to step out on my own. He was not pushy or overbearing, and we laughed a lot when we were together, but he was naturally sociable and also very practical and logical in his thinking. My excuses and fears puzzled him. Only occasionally, for a split second, would he get it — I mean really understand just how difficult something simple could be for me.

* * *

I pretend not to hear him and keep my eyes fixed on the cheerleaders making choppy aerobic movements, hoping he will give up or get it himself. My dad leans over again and cheerfully says, "Hey, Wee, here's a few bucks — go buy us some corn."

"I don't want any," I say nonchalantly. A lie. In fact, the popcorn the couple in front of us is holding looks and smells awfully good. But he reads my response for what it is — an excuse — and now he's on the trail of a potential teaching moment. Realizing I am trying once again to avoid a situation, he is determined to make me follow through and face my fear. My heart starts pounding and I feel self-conscious and weak. I know now it's only a matter of time until he wins. I am trapped.

"Come on," he urges in a sort of gentle pleading voice. "Then get some for your mom and me."

There's no escape. I don't have any reasonable excuse, and I only look ungrateful and unhelpful if I don't do it. I look at the man who has switched into his "teaching a lesson" mode and I can't explain to him how terrified I am of something this simple. He doesn't understand. Instead, he thinks this is good for me, this is a lesson I must learn and will be the better for. Dad thinks he is helping me, that this will be good practice since I never do these things, not even for myself. Any explanations or excuses I might try to offer will be dismissed, scorned. He assumes that my troubles are all in my head, doesn't acknowledge how real they are for me, doesn't validate them. Instead, he works to resolve them, believing it is better to minimize, avoid, and not feed into my ridiculous fears.

I make one last-ditch effort, which is more of a stalling technique. "I don't know where to go."

"It's just down there." He points down toward the walkway leading to the right of the stands.

Silently and tensely, I take the five-dollar bill he gives me and make my way to the food stand. I feel instantly exposed, as if everyone is staring at me, judging me. Everyone is noticing how different I am from them. How I don't belong. I try to look cool and calm as I walk the length of the hallway to the concession stand where perky female classmates fill cups with soda and squirt mustard and ketchup on hot dogs. The whole time I feel as if I am on display. Not sure what to do with my hands, how I should look, which way to go. I end up standing in a long line of people. Everyone around me feels impatient and pushy, as if they see right through me, as if they are all watching me. I can almost hear all of their impatient inner voices in my head — and somehow I feel responsible.

I finally get to the counter. My nerves are vibrating. I ask for the popcorn. I can barely look her in the eye, this goddess of teenage normality. She tells me the price and I'm not sure if the five I have is enough. I hand it over, watching her for any readable sign that I haven't given her the right amount. She glances at it and, simultaneously, I receive the box of popcorn from another girl. I feel such a wave of relief all I want to do is get back to my seat.

I walk away, weaving through all of the high-school couples, past groups of my classmates sitting and talking. I make my way back to my parents, sitting in the crowd. I hand my dad the box and return to watching the game.

Minutes pass as I observe a group of my friends from school sitting together in the bleachers below doing the wave and laughing. I don't really want to be sitting with them, but I can't help making comparisons. Somehow I feel like I don't measure up. They seem so happy, so free, so caught up in the moment — so many things I am not, couldn't be. Instead, I sit with my parents. It's the only place I want to be. In fact, my parents are the ones who dragged me to this game — otherwise I never would have come.

"Hey, Wee," I hear my dad's voice again, "where's the change they gave you for the popcorn?"

"There wasn't any," I respond, unconcerned.

"What? Noooooo!" my dad says, smiling and holding out his hand for the expected money.

"There wasn't any," I say again, with a sterner emphasis to convince him that I'm not joking.

"But I gave you a five-dollar bill. The popcorn only costs a buck."

"There wasn't any!" I repeat back to him with frustrated emphasis. "I gave the girl the money, and she didn't give me any money back."

"But she should have given you four dollars back."

I could feel myself begin to smolder and flush with embarrassment. "I didn't realize. . . . I didn't know. . . ." I stammer, a stab of fear striking with the realization that he might make me go back to the stand and ask for his change. How could I have been so stupid? What would everyone think when they found out I forgot to get four dollars in change? Now they would all know how dumb I really am. They would all see how much I don't belong. I couldn't have felt more embarrassed.

My dad reads my expression for a moment and it feels as if he is seeing me for the first time. Something changes in his face and voice. As if he feels remorseful. I watch him retreat from his "teaching a lesson" strategy. He completely backs down. I'm not going to volunteer to go get the change, but he doesn't ask me to either. Instead, he drops the whole issue and refocuses his attention on the game. I am shocked by his change in attitude and that he has given up so easily. It takes a few minutes for reality to sink in that I won't have to go back and ask for the change. I sit quietly in my seat for the rest of the game and do what I can to forget.

During this same time period, word of the book had spread. Many of my friends and classmates were curious, but I maintained my policy of keeping most of it to myself unless I was asked, and I always treated the whole experience like it was just an everyday thing, no big deal. It was already hard for my peers to relate to me. Why make it harder? I would sometimes miss a day of school and fly somewhere to speak and do interviews, but I rarely talked about it with my friends. Sometimes I felt very lonely as I listened to them recount the events of their weekends, while I felt I couldn't share my experiences without alienating myself from them.

In fact, most of my interactions with classmates in high school were in adult roles. I was stage manager for the high-school musicals. In that role, I had to interact skillfully with the adult directors while maintaining an authoritative role with the cast. For any choir events, I was usually put in charge of set design or costumes. Generally, I spent a lot of time alone and I comforted myself more than ever with the idea that I was different and special and more mature than other students. I used these thoughts as an excuse to separate myself from everyone.

Falling for a Dream

DURING MY SOPHO-

more year of high school,

my mom began researching

colleges and how they handle

learning disabilities. For me,

just getting into a college —

any college — was going to be

a challenge, considering my test

scores.

On my PSAT I scored in the ninety-third percentile for verbal skills and in the fifth percentile for math. I also lacked the math, foreign language, and science requirements usually needed to be considered by colleges for admission.

Mom bought the *Peterson's Guide to Four-Year Colleges* and urged me to start looking, anyway. At first, I didn't want to think about college and the future. It took constant prodding before Mom convinced me to delve into the phone book–sized Peterson guide and start to highlight schools I might be interested in attending.

My mom also began calling college admissions offices, researching just how receptive they were to working with students with learning differences. Some were open to it, even welcoming. Others were anything but inviting. After hearing my mom describe my challenges and abilities, one of the admissions counselors at a prestigious school responded indignantly, "I'm sorry but our students are perfect in all ways. I don't think we would consider your daughter's application."

During spring break of my junior year, we visited sixteen colleges, a family road trip that ended with just one school in the running: Kenyon College in Ohio. It was small and had a strong writing program, and the school seemed willing to accommodate learning disabilities. However, it felt almost too isolated and a little intimidating. We decided to take another trip, this time in the summer before my senior year. Tour guides, sports complexes, dormitories, green lawns, stone buildings — each campus had a different feel and look, but none of them felt just right.

I didn't imagine college would be the land of opportunity that everyone seemed to talk about it being. Instead, I viewed college as another anxiety-provoking change. I imagined the cafeteria not as a spot to meet friends, but rather as a place where I would either have to sit alone or ask others if I could sit with them. I pictured a dormitory as a loud scene, full of parties and people who would be out of control, doing things I'd never done before, with groups of people wanting freedom to play their stereos loudly or finding excuses to drink while all I wanted was peace and quiet.

I didn't particularly care about student groups on campus or where students went for coffee, or the nearby bars that were hangouts. In fact, I was afraid and intimidated by these venues of social activity. Those were places and things other people my age did — but not me. I couldn't envision myself ever being brave enough to be a part of them. I didn't look forward to having to deal with roommates, boys, parties, paying my own bills, registering for classes. I just wanted a simple, quiet, small school where I could make a few friends and go to class.

Then we found it. It was the last campus we visited, and I fell in love instantly.

Soon after our arrival at Mount Holyoke College, the student guide groups my parents and me with one other girl and her parents. We set off on the campus tour. Passing under the purplish leaves of a giant beech tree, we find ourselves surrounded by old buildings of warm red stone, which block out the noise from the road and most of the world beyond them.

The tour continues through the library, classrooms, art building, museum, theater, gymnasium, past two serene lakes connected by a gurgling creek with aging arched bridges and a waterfall that etches its way in white streams down a natural staircase of black slate, a hill covered in trees. We wander through the student center then out across the lawn toward one of the dormitories.

The dorms have the look and feel of old houses. There are a few cinder block dorms around the edges of campus, but these redbrick buildings near the campus center each have a different look and feel about them — each one unique, each projecting an aura of a former era.

Our guide explains that each dorm has its own dining hall and kitchen, which makes it possible to grab food in your pajamas, and every night at 9:00 they open up the kitchen and put out milk and cookies.

Inside a dorm room, sunlight streams in through wavy old glass, leaving a warm rectangle of light on the honey-colored wood floor. The windows are irregularly spaced. There is a wonderful creaking age to the room. A window seat in one set of windows adds to the atmosphere of nooks and crannies. This is a room that I could really call my own. I turn around and around, barely able to contain my excitement. This is it! I am in love! Here it is — as if my inner fantasies, my imagined world had become reality. I could merge my imaginary life of drawing rooms and eighteenth-century heroines with the old-world rooms around me.

I try to contain my feelings of excitement and relief during our return to the admissions office. Here is a place where I won't have to face the embarrassment and anxiety of eating meals in a huge dining facility and having no one to sit with. Here are intriguing dorm rooms, the kind I've dreamed about. The whole environment plays on my love and sense of history. There is so much beauty, it's dream-like, fantasy-like. The campus has a quiet, serious feel and there aren't any rowdy fraternity houses on its fringes. The fact that it's a women's college reassures me that I won't be faced with pressures to always drink and party.

We return to the admissions building and I am whisked into an office for my interview. I walk into my interview confidently. After all, I have done this a million times before and actually feel excited about showing off my interviewing skills. The admissions counselor asks me how I feel about attending an all women's college and shares some information about the school. She then asks me to talk about my learning disability and how I will need help. I also tell her about the book I wrote and the public speaking I have done. She looks impressed, but it's hard to tell.

Later, we meet with an education and psychology professor regarding the college's programs for students with LD. He confesses that some students have been successful, while others have struggled or even dropped out. However, there is support for learning-disabled students on campus, including two advocates who are assigned to help. He explains about course waivers and alternative course credit options to substitute for math and foreign languages. They have provisions for untimed tests and offer the assistance of note-takers and readers to those who need them. After talking with him, I am convinced that this college is the place for me.

I feel a surge of excitement and relief. Some people had told me that when you find the right college, you will know it. And I do! I will make this place home. This will be the castle in the sky I am looking for — the answer to all my problems. This is where I will finally fit in, where I will no *longer feel alone. This is where I will make friends who are like me, and who understand me. Getting through the last part of high school was going to be easy with Mount Holyoke to look forward to.*

I decided to apply early decision to better my chances of getting into Mount Holyoke. With the hope of making up for my odd test scores — and my even stranger high-school transcript that was missing most classes colleges look for, such as algebra, chemistry, French, physics, and calculus — I put together a portfolio of information to send off with my required application.

I wrote a personal statement to give the admissions committee a better understanding of my learning difference.

I sent the statement, along with a copy of *Reach for the Moon* and extra letters of recommendation from my publisher and the state superintendent of special education. I also had to complete all the other written parts of the regular application. The essay question I chose to answer began with an excerpt from a poem by Emily Dickinson, who attended Mount Holyoke:

> *Each life converges to some centre*
> *Expressed or still;*
> *Exists in every human nature*
> *A goal.*
> *Admitted scarcely to itself, it may be,*
> *Too far*
> *For credibility's temerity*
> *To dare.*

Applicants were asked to "Examine your own centre, your sense of self or your sense of purpose, in a way that illuminates, to us and to you, who you are."

Here is my essay:

Sometimes on winter mornings, I try to see myself in gathered wrinkles, my dark hair forsaking me to silver. I try to see my hands traced by blue veins and my eyes in vintage brown. I try to see myself a little bent, a little withered. I close my eyes and see me all in white, all in gray, draped in the webs of age.

Oh, I will ache a little and have one of those chronic coughs. I will sit in my chair and pull at curtains that reveal a window etched with white doves of frost. Then, maybe just then, I will know what I was and who I am. I will know all that I took and all that I gave.

It is here that I want to be a messenger, a courier of everything I've gathered. I want to tell my grandchildren of the games my friends and I would play. I want to pass on the legends that creep around us. I want to tell them of the sand dunes and of the lakes. I want to tell them of the many ghosts that look fondly upon them. I want to say that I have made a difference. I want to give them the world through my eyes.

However, for now, my center, my sense of self, my purpose is yet unclear to me. I see it like one sees a fish in a river, only silvery flashes of fin and tail. Never seeing all of it at once. The journey to discover these things lies ahead. When I am in the November of *my life maybe then I will understand my June. I do know that I want desperately to understand what I don't, and give the understanding of what I do to others.*

Perhaps one day, after I have sunken into the shadows, my grand-daughter will read one of my poems to her daughter, or show her a book that I collected, maybe even pass on one of the stories that I told. Then, there in that moment, is all that we can ever hope to be. That one little niche in time, when what we gave, or passed on, is given again.

I was excited and eager whenever I thought about college and talked about it incessantly with friends who were also busy with their application process.

I felt elated when my acceptance letter from Mount Holyoke arrived. I was so ready to leave my life and high school behind for the new world I imagined waiting ahead for me! I sat in the high-school cafeteria with my friends watching big snowflakes fall outside the windows and felt as if spring and graduation would never come. I spent the rest of my senior year stage-managing the musical, building sets, studying, hanging out with my friends, and imagining what things would be like next year.

High-school graduation did not feel like much of a celebration. Regardless of my academic issues, I never once doubted that I would graduate. My family attended the event and cheered me on. Yet, although it was my personal success, in many ways we were celebrating our family achievement together. I would never have made it without their support.

Knife, Fork, and Spoon

AFTER GRADUATION, IT

was time for me to begin

looking for a summer job. A

family friend for whom I

had often baby-sat owned an

upscale restaurant, a favorite

of the wealthy summer crowd,

and offered me a job as a

busser.

I would have to prove myself, he said, but within the first couple of weeks I should make tip pool (meaning I would share in the pooled tips of the waitstaff) and be able to gather together a significant amount of money to put toward college. Little did I know that it would be an absolute disaster.

I arrived at the restaurant early, anxious about time and not sure how long it will take me to get there. As usual, I have already completed the tasks the two table bussers on duty are expected to complete before the doors open for the evening. I have thoroughly cleaned both bathrooms and vacuumed beneath the tables and chairs in the dining room. I take satisfaction in completing these tasks, scrubbing the white porcelain of the toilet bowl, washing the sink, and hearing the gritty crackle as the vacuum sucks up tiny particles of sand and crumbs from the gray carpet. These are jobs I feel I have mastered. I can do them without fault. Knowing this helps to alleviate my guilt for all the tasks I will do wrong tonight while carrying out my normal duties as a busser.

I help two of the servers smooth the pressed white tablecloths over the square surfaces of the tables, and I make my way about the room, lighting the tea candles in their clear glass holders, a hint of sulfur and a trail of wavering reflecting flames in my wake. This part always feels as if a stage is being set.

I finish tying on the final item of my uniform, a white, knee-length apron. Now, all that is left is to wait for the first customers to come through the front doors. I feel nothing but dread and nervous tension. I do my best to block out and ignore the faintly disappointed looks of the servers when they see that I am on duty. I try to forget that it's halfway through the summer and I still haven't been placed on tip pool, while every other busser, most younger than me, has. I am barely making enough money to justify the gas to get to the restaurant, let alone enough to put aside for college expenses.

The night is a busy one, every table full. I move quickly to reset a table but I forget the salt and pepper shakers. As I reach to get them, the server I am working with moves by and mumbles that four tables need water. I go for the pitcher of water and I am stopped by the hostess who tells me that I reversed where the knives and spoons should be placed on the last table I set, and she had to move them herself after she had seated the customers. I barely feel guilty or apologetic anymore, just numb. I begin to refill water glasses. When I finish, I help to clear a table of four, bending at the knees to get under the heavy tray. Then I am asked to make more coffee.

I take the tray in and stand in front of the machine, a jumble of instructions running through my head. I awkwardly complete the task as best as my muddled mind will allow, then hurry to carry out a tray of dinners for another server. I go to get the water pitcher again and am stopped by a server who asks if I was the one who made coffee last, because someone forgot to put a filter in the machine and it has leaked all over the kitchen. She doesn't give me time to respond. No need. She has already angrily pushed her way back into the kitchen to make a new pot. Tears well up and sting the bottom of my eyelids. I push them back, telling myself I will just have to ask someone to help me with the machine next time, not dwelling on the fact that this will be my fifth coffee screwup in the last two weeks.

The other busser moves along with the traffic impeccably. She silently and quickly carries out her tasks, filling water, assisting staff, anticipating *what they will need before they even have to ask for it. I hear her compli-mented by the hostess and other staff, and I am envious of her cool compo-sure and ease. I am amazed at how she keeps it all straight, remembering all the steps in order, her speed and efficiency. I fall so short. I want nothing more than to please, but can't seem to. Instead, I have three tables to reset, two parties waiting at the door, and no time for me to accomplish any of it. Meanwhile, the hostess has to fill water glasses at two of my tables, and an-other server has to help bring tea to my table when she should be taking or-ders at her own.*

The night finally ends, and I drive home around midnight. I walk in through the back door and answer the sleepy voice of my mother who al-ways asks, "Is that you?"

"Yes," I whisper back. I climb the stairs, my feet aching, and relish the relief of taking off my shoes and untucking my shirt. I crawl into bed, but don't fall asleep. Instead, I find myself reliving the night, processing it like a videotape in my mind. Every mess-up, every mistake, runs through my head again and again as I try to figure out what went wrong, try desperately to make it right, try to remember how to do it better next time. I toss and turn, the pace of the restaurant staying with me long after the tea lights have burned themselves out, and the last half-empty coffee cups and wine glasses have been cleared for the night. I try to forget that I have to go back again tomorrow.

Desperate for money to help pay for school, I was forced to take another job that wouldn't conflict with my night job and wouldn't require that I work a cash register or deal with numbers. After frantically looking, and being turned down because most places had already done their hiring for the summer, I finally got a job at one of the hotels in town, cleaning rooms.

In the hotel room, MTV blares on the television. I can hear it over the noise of the vacuum as I kneel on all fours and wipe down the tile-lined floor with a clean rag in an attempt to remove every last hair. In the other room, I hear the vacuum roar cut off abruptly as Pat pulls the plug from the wall and begins to coil it around the back of the machine. Its wheels squawk as she drags it out to the cleaning cart in the hallway. Pat is in a hurry today. She has a date tonight with a trucker she met at the Shell station where she works nights. She is one of the five full-time cleaning women at the hotel, and has been for five years.

We have been working full speed since early morning and have agreed to go without lunch in order to finish the five rooms we have left. Two of the rooms on our list are suites that have endless miles of porcelain to wipe down and two king-sized beds with two very heavy, very wide king-sized mattresses to lift and tuck and walk around.

I work here from 7:30 A.M. until 3:00 or 4:00 P.M. and then I run home, take a shower, and leave for work at the restaurant at 5:00 P.M. Even though there are some days where my schedule isn't doubled up so I work both jobs, it has been a grueling schedule to keep. But I need the money.

I find that even though I am performing tasks I have done a million times over, I still have to give this job my full concentration. In fact, I struggle every day with simple things, like remembering to leave soap in the bathroom or leaving the right number of towels. Sometimes I forget a step, like dusting or taking out the garbage. My brain constantly feels scrambled. Already today, I have forgotten to put trash liners in one room and to wipe off the balcony furniture in another. I can hear Pat heave a heavy sigh and shake her head at me, as our supervisor makes the round of this last room and finds that I failed to replace the towels.

I grab the forgotten towels from the cart and quickly walk back to the room while Pat pushes on ahead down the hall. I feel my temperature rise and a wave of frustration wash over me. Why can't I do it right? Between this job and the restaurant, I am beginning to feel like I am buried under a heavy weight that I can't seem to crawl out from. No matter how hard I try, I can't get it right. I feel like a failure.

Midway through the summer, I sank into a deep depression. I didn't smile anymore. I didn't laugh. Nothing seemed funny. I felt worthless, drained, inferior. No matter what I did, it seemed I did it wrong. Life was an arduous, exhausting task that I had to get up and endure — not something to be lived or enjoyed.

I wondered, *What is this roller-coaster ride I am on? When will it end? Why can't I just be normal? Why does everything have to be so hard?* And now I was going to go off to college and live on my own when I was still afraid of driving myself somewhere alone. I slipped toward despair.

Mom and I sit in the van, which is parked overlooking the wide curve of the bay. The late August sky is gray and heavy with clouds that hang dramatically over the turbulent gray water, and whitecaps whip up with the strong northwesterly wind. I leave in a week for college.

She is worried about me and knows the two jobs I worked this summer were hard. She notices that I am silent more often and I smile less. I don't seem myself. She tries to reassure me and remind me of the things I do well, such as the speaking I did this past year, or the sets I built for the musical. She reflects that the negative restaurant experience was mostly the owner's fault — and my learning difference; that I was really good at baby-sitting. She sounds convincing; perhaps she is trying to persuade herself as well as me. But the heavy weight just hangs here, making it hard for me to breathe.

I stare out over the wide stretch of water and sky, at the beautifully tilted curves of land that heave alongside the shore. I feel so defeated, so numb. No matter how many times I am reminded that I am about to attend a prestigious college, or that I had a book published, or have given keynote presentations at national conferences, it doesn't matter. I still feel inadequate. It doesn't matter that I had successfully stage-managed a musical that year or had won awards at my high school. All that matters are the knife, fork, and spoon — the pieces of silverware I couldn't remember where to place. The simple steps I couldn't carry out to make coffee; the forgotten bars of soap and trash can liners; always feeling like more of a hindrance than a help. I ask my mother as hot tears run down my face, "What am I going to do if I can't even bus a table or clean a hotel room?"

The next week I left home for college.

THE TURN

I loathe change,
never wanted the turn.
It would mean I'd have to shift,
pull through the loam,
break soil's crust.
I would have to grow,
stretch an arrow's truth
to the sun.
Seek ancient arteries,
swell with water.
Unfurl leafy tarps,
hold them firm with stakes of stem.
Release the bee,
host aphids,
be plucked at,
pieces of me woven in a sparrow's nest.
Hold clusters of moth's eggs.
To wither,
be laced with brown.
To roll back,
leaving seeds to an unknown planting.
To shrivel, and starve,
grow dense and pulpy.
Back to the asylum of the earth.
To have been so much,
then nothing.
The change,
transformation,
the turn.

Seeking Lonely Places

DESPITE MY ANXIETY, I

arrived at Mount Holyoke ea-

ger and excited. Everything was

new. I felt like a giant sponge

soaking up a profusion of words,

gestures, directions, buildings,

smells, landscapes, conversations.

The first two weeks of school were overwhelming academically and full of awkward moments socially. However, I was determined to make this work.

Right away, I began meeting with the learning disabilities coordinator. We talked about my schedule and which classes he felt would be best for me. He advised me on which professors were more understanding of learning differences than others and we talked about which course waivers I should petition for. I would need a course waiver for math, and I would have to agree to take two semesters of science in its place. He also recommended that I take a test to determine my ability to learn a foreign language in the traditional way it was taught. He explained that students who have a sequential learning disability like mine usually struggle with or fail foreign-language classes. My score on the test would determine if I could petition the academic board for a foreign-language waiver as well.

My first semester course load was light. We had decided that I should start out slow, with three classes. I enrolled in an African history course, a drawing class, and first-year English. The foreign-language aptitude test showed that I had only a five percent ability to learn a foreign language — one of the lowest scores the LD advisor had ever seen. I petitioned for and received a foreign-language course waiver allowing me to take two cultural immersion courses instead.

The first semester was busy, but as college life settled into a routine, for the most part it was manageable. Gradually, a friendship network began to develop in the dorm. Most of the friends I made my first year were women who lived on my floor.

Every day was full of new challenges, and nights were spent hanging out in various friends' rooms, telling stories and laughing. Once in a while, my friends would decide they wanted to go out — go to a dance on another campus or to a club in Northampton or to a concert. Whenever I was invited, I always felt that familiar wave of insecurity and discomfort, and I would decline, making up an excuse for why I couldn't go. I didn't have enough money, or I had homework to do, which wasn't always a lie. But even as I begged off, I always knew that I could have figured out a way to join them, if I had really wanted to go.

Second semester, my involvement in the social scene continued to deteriorate. My friends came back from break ready to explore new relationships and find new places to have a good time. I was invited to parties and dances more frequently, but my reactions were always the same — anxiety and insecurity — and my excuses continued. I had a paper to write, or I would go to the library at the last minute so my friends couldn't find me and make me come with them. I spent many Friday and Saturday nights alone among the library stacks. Sometimes, when friends came by my room, I would pretend I wasn't there, ignoring their knocks. I even turned off my lights, so it looked as if I wasn't home or was asleep. There I was, sitting in the dark, trying to figure out what I would tell my friends the next morning. I felt more and more ashamed of my aversion to doing things that everyone else saw as fun.

I grew more and more isolated. At breakfast, while my friends relived funny things that happened at a party or dance the night before, I would sit silently, unable to follow the conversation, left out of their inside jokes. Some of my friends got frustrated with me and gave up inviting me altogether. I knew they complained about me behind my back or wondered or worried about me. In my habitual style, I retreated, comforting myself with the same ideas I used in childhood, that I was different, special, older, wiser, that parties and dances were beneath me somehow. I told myself that my friends just didn't understand, that I didn't need them to understand. I had been alone like this before, I was accustomed to not being a part of the social scene.

My academics also began to slip. I tried a full course load second semester — four classes — and found myself buried in work. It took me two or three times as long as my friends to complete papers and do the reading for my classes. I still lacked a sense of time, which was a difficult challenge, accentuated in college because there was no Mom or other external cues to help me plan and pace myself. If I had a paper due in four days, I had no idea how long four days was, or how long it would take me to write the paper, so I would work and work on it until it was finished, convinced that I didn't have time for hanging out with friends. I began to spend inordinate amounts of time in my room in front of the computer.

There wasn't any balance in my life. All I could think about was getting through the year. Every night before bed, it became a ritual to cross off that day from the calendar next to my pillow and then let my eyes drift to the bottom, taking notice of how many days were left before the month ended and I could move on to the next.

Although I spent days working on my papers, I could never get a grade above a B. My content and ideas were always praised, but my grammar and spelling were so poor that my grade was always dropped. I also had a lot to learn about how to write a college essay. I became impatient with myself. I decided to use the services of proofreaders at the writing center, but that required scheduling appointments. My papers had to be ready at least a day ahead of everyone else's so I would have time to make corrections. It was also nerve-racking to have my overall grade on a paper dependent upon the quality of my proofreader, which varied from visit to visit.

That spring, I began to have panic attacks again. They started out mild at first, small tremors of anxiety, a sudden upset stomach. I dismissed them as a fluke. However, it wasn't long until they became more frequent and intense, eventually launching into full-blown nighttime attacks. What took years to build to its most severe level in seventh grade, happened now in only a matter of weeks. They were back. I was losing control of myself again.

My worst nightmare had come true. I thought I had figured out the answer to my panic problems, but here they were again. I got my learning disability diagnosed. I took care of that. So why was I having them again? Now, just like before, they began to take control of my life, dictating how much and what I ate, where I went, what I participated in. I felt confused and frightened. I couldn't imagine what would make them go away this time.

Something isn't right. Feeling and consciousness come drifting up from sleep, my eyes remain closed. I try to shut my mind off again, but it is awake now and probing. I sense it, the tight acidic ball in my stomach. Is it there? Is it really there or am I imagining it? How long has it been there? Is my stomach upset? Did I wake up because I am going to be sick? I was asleep, wasn't I?

I try to ignore the sensation but my muscles begin to tighten in my legs and in my arms, and trying to relax only makes them feel worse. I try to keep my eyes closed. I swallow hard and the pit in my stomach doesn't go away, but instead becomes even tighter until I can't ignore it. My brain screams that it is real, that I really might get sick this time.

I lie very still, my muscles spasmodically tensing and relaxing, and I get a dry taste in the back of my throat as I work to sit up a little more in my bed and get my pillows raised up underneath my head. Everything is very, very still. I turn my head to look at the time. The blaring red letters say it's 3:00 A.M. My stomach contracts, and the fear of getting sick hits me in waves. This is how it would feel, *I tell myself.* This one could be real. *My leg muscles begin to tremble, shaking uncontrollably. A rush of panic and terror washes over me.*

My roommate, Erica, is asleep in the bed across from me. Her back is to the room and she is motionless. I don't want her to know — I don't want anyone to know or find out. I have my exit all planned. But these things aren't controllable. I might not make it to the bathroom in time. If only I can get this feeling to go away. If only I can stop shaking. Cool, cool water is the only thing I know to try, but it isn't foolproof. I force myself to stand on my trembling legs and the spasms slow a little, allowing me to walk. I silently move on bare feet to the mini-fridge in the far corner of the room. I move so Erica won't hear me, so she won't wake. My stomach feels sickened in waves.

I crouch on the floor and pull open the door, reaching in for the container of water I keep there. I suck in a deep breath to relieve the pressure I feel inside. For a second, there is relief, and then, as the air leaves my body, the pressure feels sickeningly worse. Unscrewing the top of the water bottle, thread by wide thread, I lift it to my lips and drink. I wait, riveted to the cold liquid's icy burn as it pours down my esophagus into my stomach. I imagine it there, unknotting things a little, the muscles forced to deal with the liquid. I know this is the telling moment, that the water will force my stomach to reveal its full or empty state. If full, there will be impending embarrassment, shame. If empty, then I am saved, there isn't anything for me to worry about. I kneel on the floor like an accused being, waiting, unbreathing, for my sentence. All of my focus is directed at the sensations within me. As if by habit, without looking, my hands unerringly twist the lid back on the container, place it back into the fridge, and close the door.

I look over at Erica's still form and then, like a bubble rising up in a pool of water, a tiny delicate sign of life bursting on the water's surface, I think I hear and feel an almost indiscernible gurgle inside my chest. I creep back across the floor to my bed and sit there for a moment, not yet ready to make the call. Then there's another gurgle, this one larger, and the pressure, the undefined knot in my middle, melts into a familiar, comforting twist of hunger. I am not going to get sick! Right now, right here at this moment, it's the most wonderful feeling in the entire world.

My constricted muscles relax. My thoughts begin to wander, my eyes move across familiar objects in the room. I lay my head on my pillow and pull my down comforter back over me. The faint imprint of my body heat settles over and around me.

I look up at the painting hanging on the wall above my bed, into the lonely and wondering face of the Lady of Shalott as she pushes off from her castle prison. She loosed the chain, and down she lay, I recite in my head, watching her long auburn hair catch the wind of the storm beginning to surge around her. Far off the sunlight is eclipsed by clouds and the river water, black and still, disappears in the eventual direction it will carry her. My head begins to feel heavy, my body relaxed. I turn over on my side, reassured by the empty feeling inside, and all becomes very dark.

Depression makes you seek lonely places, and that is what I started doing during the second semester of my first year in college. The black creek, the woods, the empty fields, the old cemetery — anywhere away from people, away from their critical eyes; I would seek out these places, choosing routes and times that would mean I could avoid as many people as possible.

My solitary walks became an obsessive need, an escape, for me that spring. Letting my mind drift, I kept scrap paper in my pocket, and sometimes I would write pieces or poems connected to my moods and experiences:

Loneliness compresses the ribs,
is gulped out in vaporous smoke.
The snow stretches out on all sides in seamless white
and the forest has lost its breathing, its movement, its sound.
Here on this silent rising hill covered in trees
I am the hope of something.

Sometimes I would write papers in my head as I walked, or introspectively analyze my behavior, thoughts, and feelings.

The long slits of early morning gray light slicing through the blinds guide my way across the area rugs and patches of cold tile floor to my closet doors. Quietly grabbing my clothes, I turn toward my roommate's side of the room. All that's visible is a curled mound of vine-covered comforter and a few strands of hair. Unmoving. Once again, she appears undisturbed by this ritual I follow, morning after morning.

I bend down, the slight cracking of my knees sounding like fireworks in the absolute quiet of the room. Grabbing my shoes and coat, I take hold of the wide, cold metal knob of the door and methodically turn it, sensing the subtle undulation of each ball bearing clicking past in a smooth quiet rhythm. I pull the door open just wide enough for my body to slip past, and then I just as quietly pull the door closed. As I release my hand from the knob, I feel my breathing come a little easier. Here, outside my dorm room, I collapse to the floor and pull on my socks and shoes, tying one and then the other.

For a moment, I stand and stare down the long corridor, past the receding rectangle of doors to the narrow lattice window that projects an eerie, glossy reflection rippling over the tiles. All appears still and unmoving, the entire dorm a catacomb of sleeping bodies. I move in silence down the hallway toward the fire exit door, so far unseen, undetected. Pulling the door open, I descend down the four flights of stairs at an increasing speed, bursting through the ground-level doorway and out into the gray morning.

I move quickly, smoothly, as fast and as wide as my legs will stride me forward, down the hill, along the path. My eyes take in the creek that slides away into the shadows of the trees, the castle turret of the dorm up on the hill, the low heavy ceiling of sky, the pavement still wet from last night's rain, and I soak up the melancholy beauty that surrounds me. I feel a million poems everywhere, but don't have the heart to bring them to words. Here in the early quiet, all this beauty feels utterly lost and forsaken, and I feel as if I belong here, lost and forsaken as well.

Some unspeakable inner need craves this solitary movement. Walking seems the only action that might generate a spark that could recharge my burned-out battery. My watchful animal instinct to avoid people is almost overpowering. When I am with others, I feel as if I am under a microscope, as if every inch of me is being scrutinized all the time. I feel sickeningly self-conscious. The only time I ever feel like I can fully let my guard down and be completely free is when I am alone. Walking. Thinking.

Why? I ask myself. Why? My pace quickens. Why am I so different from everyone? Why don't I like to go to parties? Why can't I just be like everyone else? My arms move more quickly at my sides and my focus narrows from the outside of me to the inside. Why do I keep having these panic attacks? Why doesn't anyone understand me? *My pace picks up and I can feel my heart begin to pound in my chest.* I'm not like the rest of you. I never was. I feel things more deeply, more intensely. I see the bigger picture when others don't. Why? Why?

If I just walk fast enough and hard enough, perhaps I can walk myself into answers — into understanding why my panic attacks have returned, why I can't relate to my friends anymore, why my inability to connect no longer bothers me. I feel like such a small person, so out of it, so separate, so behind.

I move along the base of the wooded hill, turn up an old two-lane track, lost in leaves and fallen branches, and begin my climb. I choose this path to the other lake because it means I can escape from the view of people in passing cars or other walkers. Once I am surrounded in the shelter of the trees, I am invisible, and my self-consciousness eases a little. I feel hidden from the world. I look down through the forest, wishing that I could disappear into these woods, become transformed into a tree or a rock. I feel incredibly, profoundly lonely. I sit down for a moment, letting the sweat cool my back. Looking out over the scene, I tell myself there is still hope for me, there is a whole world beyond this lonely hilltop that is waiting for me. I tell myself that I feel alone for a reason. That one day I will find my place.

I Can't Do This Anymore

I CALLED HOME A LOT

that spring, my mom was my

only real confidante. She was

the only person to whom I

revealed my true feelings, and

the depth of my loneliness.

Mostly this semester I had

sounded nothing but down and

miserable.

One night on the phone, my mom told me she was worried sick about me, that I needed to get help, that I should call the college counseling office and make an appointment. I agreed but put it off and put it off until one morning I hit bottom. I couldn't hold the darkness at bay anymore. I felt like I was losing my mind. I didn't care who heard or saw me. I started crying, the kind of crying in which there isn't any sound for the first few breaths. I called that day and made an appointment to see a counselor on campus. I couldn't do this on my own anymore.

I look out through the window that makes up the back wall of her office. She sits facing me. Today she is wearing a peach-colored chiffon scarf and a matching maternity dress, her heels and hose in sharp contrast to the worn blue jeans and old sweater I wear. I look forward to coming to these counseling sessions every week because I know I need help, because I need answers, and I know I can't do it alone anymore. However, every time she opens her door and discreetly speaks my name to signal she's ready for me, I always feel a little sorry I came.

It is the initial silence that is the most unbearable, the awkward silence as I walk toward her and through the entryway into her office, the forced small talk that I always start in an attempt to relieve the uncomfortable silence — the small talk that she knows is a sign I can't handle the silence, a sign to me that I can't. I'm more transparent than I would like to think.

Exhausting all my observations on the weather with little help from her, I take my usual seat, the one where I sit now, looking out the window. I feel her eyes gaze at me unabashedly, notepad in front of her, pen poised.

She rarely smiles, rarely gathers or moves her eyebrows, rarely laughs. She asks questions in a voice clear and even, revealing little emotion. In fact, she appears to be a solid rock of practiced inscrutability. Unable to be manipulated or won over, she is not here to give me her approval or friendship, but simply to listen, it would seem — listen like the white walls of my dorm room, waiting for me to fill up the silence.

I begin today's session by telling her about my friends and how I know I am losing them. I tell her how they just don't understand, how they don't get it, how they don't know what it's like for me, how I am socially forgotten. She asks me how that makes me feel. I sit quietly, flooded with emotion. But I fight it back, look at the floor searching for words I can say that will allow me to maintain control. I try reasoning it out with logic. I express my understanding of what my behavior must seem like from their viewpoint. I never go to parties or leave campus, and I always have an excuse for why I can't be a part of something. From my friends' perspective, it must seem like I am a boring weirdo — a college student who doesn't like parties and dances or trying to pick up guys, who doesn't want to go to bars, dislikes loud music, and doesn't enjoy sharing their companionship. I would probably want to give up on me, too, if I were them.

More silence follows, as if she expects me to say more, but I can't. I am determined to keep the feelings back. She asks if I have tried to explain any of this to my friends, and I say that it wouldn't matter and that no one gets it, not really, not even my family.

"I tell them that I can't tell time and they say they understand or listen and ask questions, but really they have no clue, no idea of what it's like to live without a sense of time, how that affects me every day. They can't grasp the fact that I might have to check the clock in my room a thousand times a day to orient myself; that I live with a constant buzz of anxious energy; that my whole day can be ruined by an appointment in the afternoon because I will spend the rest of the day before it feeling as if I can't do anything wrong because I don't know how long I have.

"No one understands the sinking feeling of lost helplessness when I lose track of time and the only clock I can find, I can't read. Or the anxious confusion I feel when a cashier looks into my face and wonders why I, a perfectly normal-looking person, have handed him fifty cents when he asked for seventy-five.

"They don't understand the embarrassment I feel at not being able to keep score in my gym class, never knowing how much of a tip to leave in a restaurant, forgetting how to fill out a deposit slip at the bank. Or the terrifying idea of riding a bus alone because I may not be able to figure out the schedule. Or always knowing that no matter how good my paper's content, I will get marked down for my grammar and spelling mistakes.

"Most people have never heard of the learning disability I have — dyscalculia. When they look at me or talk to me they don't think it's possible. Everyone assumes I am normal, that I can do things every other grown-up can do. I don't want to be different. I just want to fit in! I don't want to feel helpless and embarrassed or look stupid. No one really understands."

I end this long speech, my eyes looking directly at her, intent with emotion, a questioning look on my face, as if I am asking her for an answer. My speech has surprised even me. However, I know that deep down I haven't gotten to the heart of things. Deep down, what I can't admit to anyone, including myself, is that I am terrified — absolutely terrified.

The counselor gently acknowledges that I am right, and no one will ever have a sense of exactly what I go through, but that she is here to try to understand as best she can. We spend the second half of my appointment talking about my academic workload for the week, and she tries to help me lay out a plan of attack for my burgeoning assignments of papers and reading. It feels much more comfortable and safe to keep the conversation relegated to this topic. I can talk about my English papers and history assignments without bursting into tears. However, it also leaves me feeling more helpless and alone than I did before I arrived. I look at her calm face, her manicured nails, and waves of nameless feelings sweep over me. Yet I know that I can't share them, can't lose control.

Before I know it, her eyes flicker to the clock she keeps behind me, and she announces my time is up. She dismisses me just like every other client who comes in and out of her office, with her even-toned, neutral voice and smile. I leave with an appointment for next week. I make my way through the door of the campus health center, walk out under a darkening, heavy-weathered spring sky, down the narrow, paved path to the trail around the lake. I hear my feet shushing in the wet gravel as I maneuver quickly around puddles and through the trees, alert and hoping that I won't see anyone. Hoping that the descending dark clouds moving in from the west will keep everyone else inside today.

I push myself to walk as fast and hard as I can, the entire appointment running through my head. Her words, mine. Looking for the answer, still trying to figure out what I need to change or do that I am not already trying. Looking for the big answer. It begins to rain.

Not long after this walk in the rain, I come to my answer — an answer so simple and so apparent that I find myself reeling and stunned by its concise elegance.

Alone in my dorm room, I feel something aching and building inside. I try to remain focused on the glowing computer screen, the cursor, the black shapes that make up the letters, which make up the words, which make up the sentences of my literature paper. However, my eyes keep drifting, caught by the moon rising above the hill, up through its tangle of trees, sailing up, husky and full in the darkness. Henry James, I remember. My eyes move back to the computer screen and the book lying open in my lap, The Figure in the Carpet. What is the figure in the carpet? What did James intend for it to be?

There is the moon again, the dark trees, the counseling appointment I had today. I feel an internal sinking, and my eyes sting with emerging tears. I try to form the words in my mind to identify why I am about to cry, but this shift to reason and logic causes the feeling to dry up, the tears to retreat. I am left without an explanation, just the same familiar hollow sensation inside that has come to feel as much a part of me as my skin.

No one died, I didn't go to class naked, I didn't just break up with someone, or lose my best friend. My eyes move back to the computer screen, but the sinking feeling returns again and I am struck with the need to talk, to call home and talk to Mom. I pick up the phone, place the receiver to my ear, and dial my home number.

Mom answers, and at the sound of her voice, my mind packs the feeling away again. We make small talk for a moment. I am not sure what to say, how to bring it up. I don't have any words to describe or explain it.

"I've been feeling sort of strange today," I finally say. She asks me if I have been to see my counselor and I tell her that I have. She talks for a moment or two, and my eyes become transfixed by the darkness outside, my mind spins inward, the feeling swells again, and I blurt out, unable to hold it in any longer, "I just can't do this anymore." The words are out before I even begin to consciously grasp their meaning. They seem to come from some place deep within. I hadn't thought them, I felt them. With the words come instant, hot tears, and all I can do is cry.

"I can't do this anymore," I say again, and the words I had been searching for are suddenly there, effortless thoughts, as if they had been on the tip of my tongue all along. "I can't be like everyone else. I have tried and I can't do it anymore. I don't get certain things, things that some kindergartners know. There are things that are so easy for everyone else, so basic, that I don't get, and I feel like an idiot. I can't figure out how to schedule my classes. My papers are full of good ideas and sentences, but they don't get the marks they deserve. I can't balance my checkbook, don't know what a lot of money is or isn't, or how much something should cost in the store. I have a learning disability. It won't go away. I have to allow myself to be learning disabled.

"I look in the mirror and I look normal. People look at me and they see normal. I look at me and I see normal too, but I can't keep pretending. I can

say I have a learning disability, talk about it in front of huge audiences, but deep down inside I don't really believe it. I've been fooling myself. I have not accepted my disability as a part of who I am. I can't keep pretending, can't keep fighting. I'm too tired, and it's a losing battle."

Suddenly, I realize that here is the answer, simple, succinct — I have not been allowing myself to be learning disabled. I can make a thousand connections in its application to my life. I haven't been allowing me to be me. And now the truth becomes clear: When I get in over my head or my stress levels rise above my coping skills, when I ignore the fact that I need more time or extra help because of my learning disability — then I begin to have anxiety attacks. Just like in junior high, before my LD was diagnosed and I was trying to keep pace with everyone else. But once my learning disability was recognized and I got the help I needed and took the pressure off myself, the anxiety went away.

All through this first year of college I have been trying to keep pace with everyone else, not cutting myself an inch of slack — and my panic attacks returned. Now, learning from the past, I know that to get rid of the anxiety, I need to acknowledge that my learning disability is an innate part of who I am. I can't ignore it. I can't do things like everyone else at this pace. I need to slow down, get the help and support I need. It's OK to ask for help — and I'm OK just the way I am.

Despite the tears and the force of my words, I feel a huge wave of release and relief; a sense of calm and peace washes over me. I had no idea that I had been pretending not to be learning disabled. But now I see it clearly. The return of my panic attacks, the anxiety, the constant feelings of inferiority — this realization helps to explain why they came back.

* * *

Over the next several weeks, my panic attacks began to subside, but it was a slow plod to the end of the year. I couldn't wait to go home and rest.

I returned home after my first year of college reeling, exhausted, and numb. My sense of self had been dismantled. I felt disoriented — and lacked a sense of my own value, questioning my abilities and who I was. When I got home, I woke up the first couple of days and simply went through the motions without feeling anything or taking much of anything in. I knew now that Mount Holyoke was not going to be the answer to my problems, that my problems would follow me wherever I went. It was me I had to change, but I felt so weak and unsure. I doubted I would ever feel alive or extraordinary again.

Steady Progress

I NEEDED A SUMMER

job after freshman year, but

the painful memories of

work the previous summer

made me leery. My mom

found out through a friend

that there was an opening at a

local day camp.

They were looking for an art instructor to co-teach arts and crafts for campers aged six to fourteen, and also to act as a general camp counselor. I applied, got the job, and felt completely apathetic about it. Here was just one more opportunity to feel mediocre and fail, but I was used to that by now. My expectations were pretty meager when I arrived for counselor orientation in mid-June.

I met Erin that first day. She was taller and three years older than me, with short thick brown hair. I was surprised when I spoke to her — she really appeared to be listening to me. I immediately felt a sense of sincerity and thoughtfulness as well as a depth of feeling that I could relate to. She also shared a similar quirky sense of humor. I had come to feel weird and out of place with my friends at school and had begun to wonder if there was really something else wrong with me. At camp, with Erin, I felt I had found someone I could really relate to.

Erin and I unpack the camp art supplies and get ourselves settled into our square little art room. I feel a bit awkward around the kids at first. It's like learning another language and culture, another way of relating, body language, and tone of voice. I'm exhausted by the pace, the constant answering of the same questions over and over again. I learn a lot by watching Erin — the way she listens to the kids, really listens, and her ability to encourage without being forceful. There is a real, quiet intensity and thoughtfulness that Erin brings to the job. I watch and admire how she deals with discipline problems, how she calms a frustrated camper or how she sets up her explanations for the projects we are doing.

A week or two into the job, my attitude shifts perceptibly. I notice I'm no longer complaining about getting up and going to work like I had with my other summer jobs. Every day is new and different. Tasks aren't monotonous. Every day we have to dream up another project, a new way to catch the kids' interest, not to mention responding to all of the minor crises that occur all day long when dealing with kids.

For the first time in a year, I begin to feel successful again. I begin to feel like I'm good at something, at working with kids, and in using my imagination to come up with ideas and stories. My previous jobs had been repetitive tasks, jobs that called for no creativity, but instead required moving from task to task in a certain order. Now I realize that my strengths are in my creativity, my imagination, my insight into people, my communication skills. I can't remember which side of a plate to put the fork on, but I can dream up projects that will keep kids entertained all day long. When I'm allowed to run things my own way, I can be incredibly successful. I relish the awareness.

Slowly, I notice myself trickling back to life again. Erin and I continue to build a lasting friendship and spend hours together, coming up with crazy, creative ideas for projects to do with the kids. I am starting to feel a little lighter, like I'm rejoining the world.

Something else happened that summer to help me find myself again. I had been invited to participate in an educational conference at Stanford University in August. Danny Siegel, a poet, author, and lecturer, invited me to fly out to Palo Alto to be a part of his presentations. Danny is the founder and chairman of the Ziv

Tzedakah Fund, an organization that gives financial support to individuals who dedicate their lives to making a difference for others.

Sometime during my eleventh-grade year I had received a phone call from Danny. He introduced himself and talked about how much he enjoyed my book and its message, and how he wanted to include me and it in the list of people he profiled who were making a difference. I was honored.

Over the next couple months via phone calls and letters, my parents and I got to know Danny. Later that spring, he invited us to a presentation he was giving. Danny explained to us that he struggles with learning differences of his own. My book had a special personal meaning for him: When he read my story he realized that it wasn't his fault, that he wasn't less of a person. This realization changed his perspective on his own life.

I spent five days at the conference with Danny and his friends, and I was amazed by how quickly I was accepted. This acceptance gave me a sense of validation. People told me that it was OK for me to be me. It reminded me that there was a world beyond myself, beyond college, beyond my academics, in which I could fit and find my place. I was learning disabled, it wasn't going to go away, and I needed to start living my life that way. Now I had a whole group of people who believed in me.

For the first time in a long while I felt strong, clearheaded. I had a new sense of self. It made such a difference to have total strangers believe in and value me. What a gift. I returned to college for my sophomore year with an entirely new perspective. The old negative spell was broken. I knew now that Mount Holyoke wasn't going to fix all my problems. Armed with this new sense of self-control and strength, I decided to view the year as a clean slate. I didn't expect to have any friends after my behavior the previous spring, and I didn't expect it to be easy. However, I was surprised at how much more confident and comfortable I felt coming back to campus with a year of experience under my belt. So much was familiar. When we drove up in the family van I was pleasantly surprised to have my name shouted from across the lawn. It was two of my friends from my first year, who came running over to give me hugs, excited to see me, and welcome me back. What a difference it made, returning to familiar campus surroundings and getting right into classes and a well-known routine.

Based on my struggles and insights from freshman year, I made changes in the way I approached my academics. I knew my limits now and knew what I needed to do to prevent myself from losing control again. I decided that I couldn't handle more than three classes a semester, instead of the full course load of four. I also knew that I had to take action for myself to get the school to work for me. I needed to have a proofreader specifically assigned to me so that I wouldn't have to worry about whether or not I could get an appointment or have my paper completed within the writing center's hours. My LD advocate agreed it was a reasonable accommodation and arranged for a personal student proofreader, paid for by the college.

I also started using a special daily/weekly planner to help me work on understanding and managing my time so that I could strike a better balance between work and play. This simple tool — a sheet of paper with columns for each day, divided into hours by dotted lines — gave me a freedom I had never felt before. Using markers I colored in the blocks of time when I had classes and meetings. Then I blocked in meals and exercise time. When I looked at my planner, I now could see where I had white spaces: "free" time. Those precious white spaces gave me permission to relax and the reassurance that I would have "enough" time for the important stuff, time to work on homework, and time to spend with friends.

I started planning my long-range assignments by working backward from the due date, outlining tasks so that I could pace myself and get papers and projects done on time without being overwhelmed. By now, I also had a better sense of how to judge what work wasn't really necessary. Instead of reading everything suggested by the course syllabus, I concentrated on what I knew I would be held accountable for. This saved me a lot of time.

Armed with my new attitude and supports, sophomore year was dramatically different from my first year. Not only was I better able to stay on top of my classes, but I also had some fun, reconnected with old friends and made new ones.

By the end of the year, I came to the realization that even though colleges acknowledge that learning disabilities exist, the very fact they have people like my LD advocate, does not mean they truly understand the issues and needs of LD students. For me, being learning disabled didn't mean that I expected or needed my work to be made easier; it simply meant that I needed more time to do it. That meant taking a reduced course load, which made it difficult to graduate in four years. Since my family couldn't possibly afford a fifth or sixth year of college, I would have to spend my summers taking classes as well as working at a job to make money.

When I returned to college junior year, I noticed that some of the familiar patterns and people weren't there. Several of my friends had decided to study abroad for the semester or year. The rest all seemed to have found significant others or had reconfigured into new groups. Once again, I began to feel lonely and insecure, swamped as usual by the academic demands. I spent most of my nights doing schoolwork, but occasionally watching movies or reading in the library so I could get out of my room.

Most of that first semester, I was nagged by the feeling that I wasn't supposed to be at Mount Holyoke. I considered going abroad myself, fantasizing about finding a new opportunity to bond with a group of peers. I knew I had made this mistake before, imagining that by going to a new place, like college, I would finally find my place and fit in, but I had been sorely disappointed. But this time the fantasy seemed more realistic, since I would be a part of a group of people who had been thrown into a truly foreign situation together. Through sharing experiences with others in a novel environment, perhaps I would be forced to find common ground and bond.

After a lot of debate and doubt, I decided to go abroad for second semester. Because of my foreign-language issues, the key was to find a program in an English-speaking setting that was affordable and had academic classes that Mount Holyoke would count toward my degree. I also needed to find a program that would be sensitive to my learning needs and allow me the accommodations I required to be successful.

I chose an environmental studies program in Israel. The Arava Institute for Environmental Studies was based on Kibbutz Ketura in the Negev desert, thirty minutes north of the Red Sea. The kibbutz was populated largely with English-speaking people, and the program was taught in English. The goal of the institute was to bring people of different cultures and beliefs together, using shared environmental concerns as a way to help foster peace and understanding, not only in the Middle East but all over the world. The study group I was part of was made up of Palestinian and Israeli students as well as students from several other countries.

I was extremely nervous and apprehensive about going half a world away to a completely foreign environment, but at the moment, facing another semester on campus felt stifling and unbearable. Several months in Israel would provide another chance for me to experiment with building positive relationships in a group of people my age. Perhaps the shared experiences and communal living would help me find the feeling of connectedness I had known only briefly before.

I met up with another U.S. student and we flew to Israel together. It turned out that Sara was also from the Midwest, and right away we seemed to have a lot in common. I spent the first month in Israel feeling disoriented, homesick, and unsure of just what to do with myself or how to spend my time. Life got a little easier once classes began. All of the students in the program were welcoming and friendly. However, I continued to be plagued by homesickness and a vague concern that I was never going to get home again. The first few weeks I felt a little like I had landed in an alternative universe, where things happened just like they did at home, but everything, from making toast to everyday interactions with people, was profoundly different.

My dreams of making easy friendships was short-lived. Several of the students had been with the program fall semester, so they had already formed tight connections; subgroups had coalesced along gender lines, and while the women were welcoming, they didn't seem eager to fully accept new members. There was also a language barrier. Although everyone spoke some level of English, most would fall into their native tongue outside of classes, so it was hard to join in conversations and relate informally, except with the few native English speakers.

Once again, I was different. My habits were different. I wasn't interested in partying at night. I made a few token efforts to participate in the group nightlife, but I always felt like I wasn't cool enough somehow or funny enough. I was usually tired by nightfall and went to bed. Mornings, I was often up long before the rest of the group.

As so often before in my life, I found myself bonding most with adults on the kibbutz, including the woman assigned as my mentor and overseer of my independent study project. I spoke with her occasionally about the disappointment I felt at not fitting in, of suffering from the same isolation that I had back on campus. I told her that I wished that I could be young and forget the pain I knew and understood already, and maybe fit in and feel connected with other twenty-year-olds of the world. She was sympathetic and encouraged me to truly enjoy whatever people I connected with and the activities and classes I was a part of.

Eventually, I began to feel at home on the kibbutz, even started to feel more comfortable relating to some of the other students. Sara and I spent a lot of time together, walking around the perimeter fence or wandering through the clusters of houses and gardens that made up the interior of Ketura. On field trips, breaks, and long weekends, the two of us, occasionally joined by one or two others from the group, traveled to different parts of the country. I slowly realized the true value of living in an unfamiliar place, versus just visiting it as a tourist.

Poised to Enter the World

I RETURNED HOME FROM

Israel with a much wider

worldview and a conviction that

I could do anything. I gained a

real sense of confidence in my

ability to adjust and deal with

whatever situations life threw

my way.

However, not long after my return home from Israel, my mom noticed I was experiencing sharp mood swings and that I projected a down demeanor. These moods were nothing new for me — I had experienced downs my whole life and often turned to my mom to talk about them. But now she expressed her growing concern and suggested I talk to my doctor about the possibility that I might be depressed.

My doctor asked me some questions and prescribed an antidepressant. Within a few days I felt a buzz, as if someone had brightened the computer screen in my mind, turned it up a few notches. But I also began to experience insomnia, a frequent side-effect of the drug. The hours spent with my body yearning to sleep while my mind kept racing were excruciating.

I returned to the doctor, and she decided to try a different antidepressant, which seemed to interact better with my system. After being on medication for six weeks, I began to notice a remarkable difference in my life. My anxiety level diminished almost completely. Suddenly, I felt comfortable doing things I never had before, such as shopping and driving my car. I discovered firsthand the difference between being sad and being depressed. I discovered that I could feel sad and keep it in perspective, moving on with my thoughts and life rather than getting caught up in a spiraling cycle of anxiety and despair. Before, when I felt sad or down, it was all-consuming, immobilizing. Now I could respond, adapt, move forward, keep it in perspective.

Looking back, I have come to believe that I was probably depressed most of my life — at least since the fourth grade. Like the glass shower door in a soap scum commercial, my life before antidepressants was coated with a heavy gray film that colored everything — even my good times. Now the film had been washed away. My life appeared clear, bright, and in perspective. I was still the same person, but more balanced and relaxed. The semester in Israel had given me a needed break, and I returned to college for my senior year feeling more mature and confident. I reconnected with friends and jumped right into activities. There was an urgency about that final year. Plans for after college loomed on the horizon and finishing the final load of work for that year was challenging. Nearly all of my classes were three-hundred-level seminar courses, and were reading and writing intensive.

I really noticed the benefits of antidepressants one night early that fall. Several friends and I decided to go to a concert in a neighboring town. We were early, so we split up to do some window-shopping. It began to rain so the friend I paired up with and I stepped into a nearby restaurant and sat at the bar to wait for the others. I was shocked when I sat down in the crowded bar and wasn't gripped by any feelings of fear, anxiety, or insecurity. I felt at ease, confident, like I had just as much of a right to be there as everyone else.

I found myself jumping into other situations that I would have avoided before, but I now felt amazingly at ease. I went to concerts and sports events and cheered with the rest of the crowd, always surprised to find myself hooting and hollering with everyone else, letting myself get carried away in the moment — feeling normal and natural. I didn't have to work at having a good time because I truly was having a good time. I also felt much more comfortable in my friendships. I was better able to cope and roll with the punches in my relationships, and I felt less needy and dependent.

However, halfway through my first semester of senior year, my mellow attitude turned into apathy. I couldn't bring myself to do homework or really care much about anything. Nothing was a hassle or a problem, I was feeling just fine. I also began sleeping, taking long naps around the same time every afternoon. When I returned home for winter break, I consulted a psychiatrist who specializes in matching antidepressants with people. He asked a lot of questions and confirmed my depression diagnosis. He decided to switch me to yet a different antidepressant.

After taking the new drug for only a few days, I couldn't believe how well it blended with my chemistry. It didn't seem like I was taking medication, yet I felt naturally up and energized. I was also able to sleep through the night and no longer felt apathetic or took so many naps.

I can't imagine how different my life might have been had I been diagnosed with depression earlier. I recognize the advantage nondepressed people enjoy. My brother is a perfect example. His brain chemistry allows him to function normally, to be at ease in the world. Not only was I learning disabled, my brain chemistry made it even more difficult for me to function normally. Something I had spent my whole life blaming myself for and feeling ashamed of — my inability to just buck up like other people, or be social and accomplish things that are so easy for everyone else — was in part really an issue of brain chemistry. I realized that while I had to live with my learning disability, I didn't have to live with depression.

By second semester, I was completely ready to be done with college. I felt like I would never finish my final papers and projects, but the day came when I did. I was going to graduate from Mount Holyoke without a credit to spare and, to my surprise, with honors.

Classes ended and most of the seniors left campus for the two weeks in between the end of classes and graduation. Michigan was too far away to travel, so I stayed in my dorm room, waiting for my parents to arrive.

Campus was all but empty during the days I was there waiting. A few seniors had stayed, those whose homes were distant, but for the most part, campus was quiet and deserted, which gave me a unique opportunity to say good-bye. I went from room to empty room one night in my dorm, looking at all the rooms I would never inhabit. Checking out their closets and desks, looking out at their views.

Then I slipped out of the building and took a walk around campus. I had often done this at night, but tonight the campus was more empty and quiet than I had ever seen it. It felt like I was the only person left. The warm spring air felt good, and I made my tour through the lamplight and the shadows. I sat in alcoves and by trees where I had never sat before. Eventually, I found my way to an Adirondack chair positioned in the middle of the wide green at the center of campus. I leaned back in the white chair and looked up at the night sky littered with stars. What would my future be? What was next? How vast and endless the sky!

Graduation weekend arrived at last, brimming with old college traditions that mark this rite of passage for Mount Holyoke women.

It is cloudy, cool, and white-gray. The air is heavy and damp. It has been threatening rain all morning. The grass and trees are all very green in their late spring colors. My friends and I find one another and form our group. We joke and laugh, none of us believing this day is here. We chatter and I feel numb to what seems like one more requirement we have to complete before we can finally hold those pieces of paper in our hands.

We get into line, four abreast, behind hundreds of others, all dressed in white. Two long chains of laurel leaves stretch along the entire length of the line of graduating seniors, one on each side of the groups of four. On command, the women on the outside of each foursome take up the laurel chain onto their shoulders, so that the entire chain is draped from one set of shoulders to another on down the line.

The laurel parade has been a day-before-graduation tradition at Mount Holyoke for decades. The band strikes up a leisurely march and the procession begins. Arm in arm, we walk off the lawn and start across the campus, heading for the fenced-in grave of college founder, Mary Lyon. The entire route is crowded with faculty and families, all cheering as we pass, taking pictures, waving. We slowly make our way around one side of the green, only a bit more to go.

The foursomes of alumnae ahead of us begin dividing and turning to line both sides of the parade route. We start to pass them, a flood of white. My stomach flip-flops. Chills run the length of my spine. Tears ache in my throat. I am astonished at the sight unfolding before me. I finally comprehend the meaning of this ceremony and my time at this college.

At first, the faces of alums on either side of us are young faces. Only a few years older than we are, they could have been members of our class. As we progress, class by class, the faces of the women become older, gradually taking on the middle-aged features of our mothers. And then they become older still, grandmothers, great-grandmothers. Natural brown, blond, black, red hair, giving way to tints and dyes, then to silver and white. Smooth skin, tight and full, giving way to laugh lines, and then loose wrinkles. I notice that some are crying, sending knowing looks. Seeing us as the future, seeing us as they once were. All of them have completed this ceremony, all of them once were poised to enter the world, their whole lives before them. Now all of them have returned to this place to celebrate the circle of life. And I am now a part of that circle.

We begin to snake around the grave until the whole class encircles the white marble stone. We pass the laurel chain over our heads to those standing closest to the fence, and they drape the chain around its post so that it completely encloses Mary Lyon's tomb. Then we pull out a song sheet and join with the alums of all ages in serenading our alma mater.

It was at that moment, while we sang, that I bonded with my peers in a new way and appreciated what a haven Mount Holyoke has been through the years for women. I felt a part of something special, another link in the chain, connected through time.

The following day I graduated from college. After the laurel parade, this ceremony was anticlimatic. Danny Siegel made a special trip to watch me walk across the stage and receive my diploma. Afterward, my friends and I grouped together in our caps and gowns and our parents took snapshots of us in the rain.

I felt relieved it was all over and completely at a loss when I thought about what might be next.

Afterword

Through the process of writing about my life, I have remembered things I had locked away and forgotten. The difficulty with memories is that while we may not consciously remember them, they still affect our lives in the present.

It has been two and a half years since I graduated from college. I returned home without any idea of what I wanted to do with my life or what was next. My focus for so long had been just to get through school, finish all the work, get passing grades, and leave with a degree. But after graduation I could barely wrap my mind around the concept that I did not have to return to the routine of classes and homework in the fall. My time was my own.

I spent the summer trying to form some semblance of a life plan and working at the same day camp where I had spent the three previous summers. By chance I got a job that fall as a residence hall counselor at a local boarding high school. I was assigned to live and work in a all-male residence hall, which turned out to be a crash course in parenting, counseling, policing, and negotiating. I got to know myself and my own limits and strengths in ways I had never tested them before.

However, as I settled into the routine of my new job, something deep inside me started to bleed into my everyday thoughts. Something that was more feeling than words. I found myself holding back tears while carrying on a conversation about brands of laundry detergent or waiting for a stoplight to turn green. I found that my patience had dwindled, and my mind was running through images of the past more and more frequently.

I described this to my counselor, a woman I had been working with since my senior year in college. She explained that during all the years I was in school I couldn't let myself feel because it was too painful. To survive those years I had to hold my feelings back, and keep myself from being overwhelmed by fear, failure, isolation, and shame.

But now that I was done, there were no more tests to take, papers to write, or books to read—no more expectations. It was safe for my mind to unwind itself delicately down into the pain that I hadn't allowed myself to feel. And to my surprise, all the feelings were there, undiminished by time, feelings I had felt as far back as early elementary school. And what I found at the heart of it all was a little girl who for so many years had felt nothing but alone.

I still struggle with telling time, figuring out the tip in restaurants, balancing my checkbook, and understanding and counting money. I get anxious in new situations. I become lost and overwhelmed in airports and shopping malls. I feel flustered and frustrated at times, wishing my disability were a visible one so that people wouldn't be so disbelieving when I try to explain that I can't count out the change I owe them or calculate how many miles I have driven. I still have moments when I feel very small and incapable.

However, over the years I have also come to view my learning disability as a rather strange and unusual gift. I believe it has allowed me to develop strengths I might not have otherwise developed. I spent so many years as a young child honing my observation skills, learning to read the small facial gestures of people, and studying their changing moods, reactions, and patterns of behavior. I needed these skills to survive. However, now this same ability is an asset as I try to reach out and help others who are struggling. I feel a sense of awareness that I may not have had otherwise.

Through my disability I have learned the power of persistence, of not giving up in the face of pain and fear. We are stronger than we think we are. My educational journey has been anything but a linear path; I can't help but feel that it has stretched my creative problem-solving skills.

My disability has also taught me the rewards of reaching out for help. I hid so much, for so long, in isolation. However, when I finally did ask for help, a new world opened up for me. Whether it was my parents, a good counselor, medication, or the act of finally being honest with myself, all forms of help have greatly enhanced my life.

We all come in unique packages with strengths and weaknesses, and somewhere there is a precious gift in all of us. I was blessed to have parents, mentors, and teachers who nurtured mine. No matter how difficult or complex the person in front of us may be, I have learned never to stop looking for his or her gift, as those around me never stopped looking for mine.

My mentors have taught me the power and importance of giving back to others. I value each of these people immensely and I will work hard to pass on to others what they have freely given to me. I would like to encourage everyone to reach out to someone and give your time. It is that gift of time that has made such a difference in my life.

My family and I went through the full range of emotions in learning to cope with my disability. At first we felt denial, anger, isolation, fear, guilt, shame, and a whole host of negative emotions. However, when the school finally recognized my learning disability in junior high, we felt relieved and free to accept my learning disability as a part of my life. But what we did not understand was that our sense of my LD was based on what we knew about it at that time and in that situation. What high school, summer jobs, college, and the years following have taught me is that each new life situation requires a new understanding of how my learning disability will affect me. I have had to learn to make peace with the concept that I will always be working within myself to accept how my learning disability affects me as the circumstances in my life change. Acceptance is not a one-time experience. There will, undoubtedly, be more times in my future when things will become difficult again. Hopefully I will be able to draw on the lessons of the past and give myself permission to be who I am.

Antidepressants still play an important role in my life. They allow me to feel the entire range of emotions, including sadness, but don't allow me to get caught in cycles of thoughts that overpower me and hold me back. Sometimes I wonder what my life would be like had I been diagnosed with depression earlier, how different my relationships and ability to cope with my learning disability would have been. But the lessons I learned before antidepressants have been invaluable, and I am proud that I accomplished as much as I did, even with the gray film and weight of depression clouding things.

For the first time I am forming relationships that feel whole. I no longer comfort myself with ideas of my own difference and uniqueness. If anything, I struggle with the realization that I am normal, that I am, for the most part, just like everyone else.

This past summer I visited the lake where my family has a small cottage. At dusk I walked down to the shore, watched the colors in the sky drift into dreamlike hues, and saw the trees all around turn to black. I decided to slip off my shoes and wade out into the water. It struck me, as the quiet liquid inched up over my knees, around my thighs, and up to my hips, that for the first time I am really living my life. I am not just watching people from the shore, but I am swimming with them.